Anonymous

Broad Norfolk :

being a series of articles and letters

Anonymous

Broad Norfolk :
being a series of articles and letters

ISBN/EAN: 9783744767811

Printed in Europe, USA, Canada, Australia, Japan

Cover: Foto ©ninafisch / pixelio.de

More available books at **www.hansebooks.com**

BROAD NORFOLK.

CONTRIBUTORS.

	PAGE
A.B.C.	65
A.D.	63
A.G.D.	38, 41
A.J.G.	41
Alpha	63
Andrews, Herbert	72, 86
Arch Labourer, An	81
Ayers, E. T.	73, 84
Baker, S. E.	75
Barker, W. S.	36
B.B.	66
Bird, M. C. H.,	19, 34, 48, 73, 83, 94
B.O.P.	18
Bor	14
Bussey, Chas.	23
Bussey, L. A.	85
C.	95
C.C.	16
C-H.	4, 13
Clarke, S. T.	40
Clemence, J. L.	26, 80
Clericus	89, 99
Daisy Dimple	85, 88
Davies, Christopher	78
Davison, D.	70
Dowell, E. W.	49
E.	60, 92
E.E.M.	71
E.S	99
E.S.B.	97
Ex-Under-Sheriff	65
F.G.S.	86
Forster, F. R.	27, 34, 41
F.W.B.	36

	PAGE
George	71
Giles' Trip, Author of	4
H.B.	16
Het Varke	30, 78, 87
Hewett, E.	69
Holland, J.	72
Hotson, W. A.	88
J.C.S.	60
J.H.	71
J.L.	92
Joskin	28
J.R.B.	22, 32
Kendall, E.	73
Lawk-a-daisy-me	60
Literary World	102
L.J.	72
Mollie	95
Norfolk East	67
Norfolk Dumpling, A.	15, 94
Norfolk Farmer, A.	23, 25
Norfolk, A Lover of	18
Norfolk, North	39, 92
Norfolk, Old	39, 90
Norfolk Swimmer, A	74
Norfolk, West	24
Norfolk Woman, A	54
N.S	15
Octionary	5
One Interested	24

	PAGE
Patterson, A. ...	49, 52, 100
P.E.D. ..	.. 90
Perkins, J. P.	... 21
Pharaoh ...	... 62
Pitcher, J. ...	... 51
Pomeroy, E. B.	... 59
Rambler ...	... 59
Rector ...	... 65, 88
R.L.	... 67, 71
R.W.C. ...	... 13
S.	... 37
S.E.A. ...	.. 98
Shaw Leest, W.	... 69
S.J.W. ...	... 88
Skinner, E. ...	... 84
Southwell, T.	... 51
Suffling, E. B.	32, 101

	PAGE
T.C.B.	... 70
T.G.S.	74, 100
Tew Chaps ...	... 24
T. Licec	.. 97
T.P.S.	... 56
T.T.	... 63
Tucker, R. G. W.	... 25, 61
Tuxford, E. R.	... 18
Verdant Green	... 31
Watson, W. ...	... 92
W.C.S. ...	... 55
W.F.	. 91
W.H.C.	17, 20, 27, 57, 67
W.L.	... 40, 86
W.N.	... 61
W.S.	... 20
W.W.	... 85

PREFACE.

The articles and letters in this pamphlet have been re-printed almost *literatim et verbatim* as they originally appeared in the columns of the *Eastern Daily Press*. "Broad Norfolk" as a subject for discussion was first broached in that journal on the last day of 1892. Throughout January of the present year a peculiarly animated correspondence was maintained from day to day, and when the topic had practically spent itself there remained perhaps the most remarkable accumulation of provincialisms ever collected in any county in the kingdom. A complete index has been compiled of every curious word and phrase occurring in these pages. Hence it must not be imagined that the tabulated lists represent terms in common use in Norfolk alone, or even in East Anglia alone. Still, it can be said of them with safety that the words they contain form part of the colloquial dialect quite recently, if not at present, in use in the

Eastern Counties. To determine to what extent these usages are peculiar to Norfolk must be left to the philologist upon whom the mantle of Forby may fall. For myself, I need only express the pleasure it gives me to have been the indirect means of preserving in this form the scores of little "natives" which in all human probability the Board Schools will have killed in a generation.

COZENS-HARDY.

Eastern Daily Press,
    Norwich.

BROAD NORFOLK:

BEING A SERIES OF

ARTICLES AND LETTERS

Reprinted from the "Eastern Daily Press."

EDITED BY C-H.

NORWICH:
NORFOLK NEWS COMPANY, LIMITED, MUSEUM COURT,
1893.

INDEX.

	PAGE
Napping or Knapping	53
Nation	9, 74
Neesen	7
Next-day-morn	60
Nicely	24, 64
Nip along	40
Nipper	28
Noah's Ark	2
Nointer	85
Non-plush	64
Nowt	60
Numm-chance	41, 99
Olf	29
Olland	37, 54
Ollust	11
Other some	99
Out abroad	27
Out for, who is the bell	60
Pakenose	27, 58
Pakin'	14
Pample	5
Par-yard	27
Parts, To put on his	18, 64
Pawk	26, 58
Pax-wax	35
Ped	90
Pelanders	85
Pensey	99
Perk	61
Perseyvance	85
Pick cheesin'	14
Piece	28
Pightle	27, 58
Pilcochia	94
Pinglin'	41
Pin-patches	35
Pishmires	64
Pit	96
Plancher	39, 82
Plantain	59
Pogram	11, 33, 61
Pollard	84
Popple	92
Popples	92
Posset	84
Pudden-poke	7
Pulk-hole	2, 58
Pulks	77
Push	22
Putty	77

	PAGE
Quackled	27
Quaggled	68
Quant	77, 82
Quicks	12
Quick-set	84
Rafe-boards	84
Rands	15, 77
Ranny	35
Rare	25
Rattick	25, 28
Ratticker	28
Rear, In the	41
Refuge	27
Respectable	99
Ridiculous	98
Riddle	99
Riffle	14
Rig	3
Right consistent	88
Rightsides	25, 68
Ringe	61
Rise	61
Roaches	72
Rocked	25
Rockstaff	99
Rodger or Sir Roger	12, 33, 77, 82, 96
Roky	2, 63
Rely-poly	19, 21
Rootling	100
Rouding-time	77
Rum	40
Rumbustious	90
Run	27, 84
Runty	5
Sadly	21
Sag	26, 33, 59
Sales	90
Sally	84
Sammucking	24
Sammy, play	35
Sannikin	54, 62
Sarshen	54, 65
Sars o' mine	35
Sawney	68
Scald	28
Scalps	93
Scamel	74, 78, 93, 94
Schwad	55
Scocker	61

INDEX.

	PAGE		PAGE
Scrog	84	Snatchet	84
Scud	2	Sneck	52, 90
Scuppet	5	Snew	4, 52, 59, 61
Sea-pig	99	Snob	40
To see to	60	Solid	68
Sele of the day	29, 98	Sorzles	6
Sets	25	Soshing	22, 66
Settle	84	Sowse	5
Several	25	Spink	37
Shack	30	Splarr	27
Shacking	61	Spline	90
Shackled	14	Sploddin	40
Shail	59	Spoat	39
Shammock	92	Spore	25
Shanks' pony	84	Spoult	40, 53
Shanny	25	Springy	62
Sharm	23, 59	Spuffling	30
Shepherd's flock	84	Squackle	90
Shiffin hisself	89	Squeezened	27
Shornt	40	Squinder	25
Shortening	22	Squit	55
Shrubs, herbs, &c., a list of	101	Staithe	30
		Stammed	7, 23, 70, 79
Shug or Shig	27	Stand up	13, 16
Shuloe	22	Stannicle	35
Shy	21	Stingy or Stingey	14, 25
Shywannicking	74	Stitch	3
Sibbits	11, 17, 18, 19, 26, 73	Stove	63
Sidewiper	94	Strappen	5, 29
Sidus	22, 59	Stroke, Some	65
Sisserara	5, 59, 87	Stub	99
Skeins	87	Stukey Blues	86
Skeps	37	Suffin'	24
Skinker	66, 90	Sumpy	37
Skive	49	Sunk	56
Skran	55	Sunkets, Sunketing	40
Skruke	70	Swack	35
Skruzzle	35	Swacken	5
Skutes	12, 38, 59	Swad	92
Slackbaked	34	Swag	49
Slammakin	35	Swaling	59, 66
Slaver	55, 97	Swang	91
Slew	56	Swap-tub	35
Slight	90	Swared	35
Slippy	91	Swidge	6, 39
Slobber	35	Swimmers	12
Slov	92	Swiping	77
Slus	40, 59	Swish	25
Slussy hound	94	Switched	31
Smeaa	70	Swiving	37
Smoultin'	80, 94	Swop	26
Smur	2, 60		
Snaast	6	Take-on	41, 74
Snasty	12, 32, 38	Tang	84

INDEX.

xi.

	PAGE
Fosey	3
Foumart	99
Fourses	8, 14
Frails	77, 81
Frame	32
Frenched	22
Fresher or Froschy	7, 30, 38
Fribbling	60
Frimmicating	92
Frowey	27
Frummety	6
Full-flopper	84
Fungered	74
Funked	87
Funky	65
Furrin	25
Fursickin'	14, 19, 41
Fusty	58
Fye	3, 17, 87, 98
Fysty	27, 58
Gaddy-wentin'	94
Gaffer	24, 58
Gaggles	87
Gaily	24
Gain and Ungain	61
Gainer	40
Game	12
Gan (for given)	81
Gathered	62
Gatless	5
Gavvel	40
Gawky	5, 29
Gay	27, 37, 54
Gloat	77, 81
Goaf	89, 82
Gobs	6
Golder	27, 35, 73
Goms	9, 74
Good	27
Good-steward	40
Good-tidy	24, 64
Gooseberryfool	6
Gormed	9
Gorn sim your body	25
Gotch	3, 6, 15
Go-tu-meetin clothes	56
Grained	63
Greened	6
Grubbing	60
Grup	28, 36
Gruttling	91
Gulcher	56
Gum-ticklers	84

	PAGE
Hackering	88
Hake	17, 20
Half-rock	58
Hallo largess	8, 33
Hampered to get hold of	88
Hample	37
Hank	3
Hansell	71
Happened	63
Harnser	23, 57
Harwich, Ketched me all up at	41
Hasel	3, 25
Hawky	61, 77
Haze	12
Heater	88
Heel	62
Heign	3, 15, 22
Hen's polly	27
Hick-up, snick up	13
Hidlond	22
Hid-se-rag	34
Highlows	7, 30
Hike	65
Hild	72
Himpin'	12, 25, 33
Hind	84
Hinder	9, 23, 70
Hingles	66
Hobby	40
Hobby-lantern	99
Hod	84
Hodmandod	7, 30
Holger-boy	33
Holl	2, 17, 19, 22
Hoppen-toad	7, 29
Hotch-potch	84
Hough	53
Housen	7, 30
Hove	81
Hovelled	14
Hovers	19, 77
Howsomever	41
Hub-ma-grub	81
Huddren	5
Hulk	72
Hulkin'	5, 29
Hull	5
Hulvers	24, 58
Hutkin	12, 58
Huusb	85
Hyke	32
Hyvers	17

	PAGE
If so being you can't go	68
Illconvenient	25
Imitate	22, 25
Ingen	6
I 'ont het	68
Jack up	55
Jammuck	53
Jangle	72
Jannick	55, 59
Jiffey	55
Jiffle or Jidgett	55
Jill	84
Jimpsener	62
Jot	84, 86
Jowl	27
Jumble	54, 61
Kane	26, 33
Keeler	22, 35, 58
Keeping-room	31
Kichell-cakes	78
Kiderer	66, 82
Kidgy	32
Kindling	22
Kind 'o	16
King Harry	7
Kinsarm	64
Kipper	100
Kit	72
Knacker	66
Knickled	14
Know	61, 96
Krinkle	35
Lamming	77
Lamper-along	34
Larrup	27
Lash	61, 68
Layer	37, 54
Lay ferrard	34
Lay Over Meddlers	9, 28, 33
Lether	63
Lief	24
Lig	27
Liggers	77
Like-to-be	88
Lim	3
Limpsy	86
Lit	3
Living upright	90

	PAGE
Loaders	77
Lock	40
Loke	8, 53
Lollup	5
Lork-a-mercy	40
Lower	90
Lucum	84
Lug	72
Lummock	5
Main	70
Main, in the	41
Mala-hacked	53
Malkin	58
Malt	74, 93
Mardle	11
Mastrous	37
Mauled	25
Maund	100
Mawkin	14, 19, 58
Mawther	5, 16
Mavish	7, 29, 57, 62
Meetiners	56
Mendin	9
Mentle	58
Mew-heart	99
Miel-banks	77, 82
Mifflin	70
Miltz	56
Might	61
Ming	7
Mittens	7
Mocking-church	98
Moderate	25
Moise	76, 84
Molt	35
Morfrey	56
Mort	39
Mouse-hunter	99
Mother	53
Moultry	25
Mow, old sea	60, 93
Muck-crome	3
Muck-wash	97
Mucky	17, 18, 21, 25, 30, 78
Muddle	21, 92
Mung	17
Nab	19, 68
Nab-the-rust	65
Nag	99

INDEX.

	PAGE
Aainter	35
Abroad	88
Acabo, that would puzzle	68
Act	64
Alder	75
Applejacks	12
Arms and legs	72, 83
Arradeen	63
Averdupois	98
Babbing	77
Back-stalk	27, 87
Balaams-smite	54
Bannock	85
Barksel	25
Barleycorn, Ho John	83
Barm	83
Bauley-boats	77
Baulks	83
Beck	28, 75
Beetle	83
Being	16
Being one's share	29
Betsy	83
Betty Martin, That's all me eye and	66, 71
Bever	8
Bighes	12
Bile	83
Bing	22
Birds, East Anglian	41 to 52
Bish-a-barneybees	35, 82
Bishimer	62
Bloodulfs	87
Boiler	22
Boke	99
Bor	5, 38, 77
Botty	97
Brawn	7
Breakin' a bit	63
Breck	87

	PAGE
Bright	78
Brumble	83
Buffle, hull him in a	86
Bulls	66
Bullverin	100
Bunker	92
Bunny	7, 29, 85
Buskin	18
Buttress	56
Buzzle-head	68
Caddow	57
Cail	5, 59
Call, no	64
Carneying	34
Carnser	16, 17
Carpenter's Soda	63
Car woo	72
Cars	77
Catched him a rum'un	68
Cedar Pencil	78
Chance	88
Chapman	86, 87
Charley, play the	35
Cherubidin	64
Chife	41
Chitterlings	6, 29
Cholder	55
Christmas	25
Chummy	83
Chump	30
Church-hole	83
Clates	83
Click	62
Clink	23
Clip	5
Closes	26
Clout	23
Clung	41, 53, 99
Clutch	61
Cobble	83
Colder	28, 73, 77, 79

INDEX.

	PAGE
Comeback	8
Contain	57
Comforter	27
Cooshies	22
Cop	5, 22
Corder	29, 73, 77
Corker	60
Coquilles	78
Cosh	83
Cosset	8, 57
Cranky	30
Crick	66
Crimalkin	58
Crinkley-crankley	55
Crock	98
Crome	29
Crowd	5, 21
Crow-keepers	72
Crumb	27
Crumplin'	20
Crush	98
Cubbaw	57
Culch	6
Cum-harley	12, 22
Cum-hether	8, 12
Cup-bear	12, 28, 57
Cussey	85
Dabster	99
Daft	84
Dag	2, 74
Dakes-headed	85, 94
Dams	77
Dang	8, 29, 57
Danks	54
Dannies	88
Dannock	18, 60, 85
Dardle dum due	94
Darn	8, 29, 57
Da' say	67
Dead-a-Bird	2, 90
Deceit	63
Deen	6, 21
Deficiency	58
Deke	2, 10, 15, 17, 19, 20, 22, 24, 31, 35, 36, 39, 67, 75, 94
Denesquittin'	14
Dibbling	84
Dickey	8, 20
Dickey-shud	88
Dike	36, 53
Ding	32
Dingle	27

	PAGE
Do	25, 27, 37, 52, 63
Doated tree	92
Dodman	7, 30
Doke	24, 29
Donkey-legs	85
Don't	25, 27
Don't ought	53, 63
Doss	84, 85
Dotts	56
Douse-a-bit	40, 68
Dow	23, 58
Down-pin	41
Dowshie	28
Drant	70
Draw-latchin'	41
Dreep, on the	86
Driftway	29
Drug	84
Drum	65
Dudder	16, 18, 19, 21
Dudman	58
Dullor	3, 15, 20, 63
Dump	84
Dumplin dust	84
Duttin	3
Duty	27
Duzzy	14, 29
Dwils	22, 29
Dydling	77
D'you dut	88
Ear	72
Ecclester	70
Enow	24, 58
Fang	27, 99
Fare	14, 25
Fatagued	88
Fawny	27
Feeten	85
Fence	61
Ferry-fake	56
Few	60
Finnickin'	60
Fishimer	62
Flare-up	94
Flat	61
Fleet	62, 77
Fleeten	73
Flight-of-bees	84
Flopped	55
Forgive	25

INDEX.

	PAGE
Tangle-leg	83
Tantrums	6, 29
Tarnation	9
T'do	27
Tempest	21
Terrify	59
Thape-pie	86
Thew	4
Thongy	2
Thow	4, 25
Timbered	87
Time	27
Ting	84
Tissicking	26
Titchy	71
Titty	20
Titty totty	56
Titter-ma-torter	56, 81
Toad in the hole	84
Together	2, 9
Tom and Jerry shop	67
Tolc	39
Top sawyer	84
Toward	8, 22
Towney	40
Trape	27
Trapen	60
Traunce	92
Tremble	86
Triculate	12
Troll	25
Tumbler	3, 22
Tupe	27
Tupp	84
Tussock	3
Twilt	85
Twinters	86, 87
Twizzling	66
T'year	27

	PAGE
Unsensed	62
Vardle	86
Wadges	55
Wake	33, 94
Walentin' Good Morrer	83
Wamp	99
Wank	52
Wanklin'	92
Want	64
Wanten	61
Wap	84
Warp	99
Water-delf	2
Water-eynd	77
Water-shutin'	86
Wednesday, Won't get further than	25
Welt	61
Whasking	40
Wheatsel	3
Wheesh	12, 38, 57, 91
Whopper	60
Wimple-trees	37
Wind-jammers	84
Winnock	6
Without	27
Wittery	94
Woorree	8
Woosh	22, 23, 52
Wort, over	22
Yappin'	41
Yard of Plum Pudding	13
Yipper	60
Yows	23

BROAD NORFOLK.

OUR English language, in virtue of its being a living language, is periodically importing fresh words into its vocabulary as they become fashionable, and is gradually getting rid of useless and cumbersome terms. Illustrations of the latter process will occur to everybody. Examples of terms of recent importation now generally adopted as good English are such as *embarrass, chagrin, grimace, repartee*, all of which, according to one of Dryden's plays, were considered affected in the latter half of the seventeenth century. Provincial English is often treated with the most unmerited contempt, and no one seems disposed to go to its rescue. Yet after all, what are commonly set down as vulgarisms, are to a great extent, only terms used in more or less remote parts of the country by people who have not kept abreast with the advance of the language. The man who speaks broad Norfolk, for instance, is at once stamped as below the mark in intelligence; but the genuine Norfolk countryman is justly entitled to boast that he is never guilty of the unspeakable vulgarism of the townsfolk, who are seldom so happy as when they are running amuck amongst the h's. Our own county of Norfolk can boast of a prolific vocabulary of provincialisms; types, for the most part, as philologists tell us, not of bad but merely of antiquated English. Several illustrations suggest themselves to me; scores of others no doubt will readily occur to readers who have seen the inside of a farmyard or come across a typical agricultural labourer.

The words *dag, smur,* and *scud,* employed to mean a driving drizzle of rain, are all provincial, if they are not peculiar to Norfolk. *Dag,* it is worthy of note, once signified a dew, whilst *scud,* in its legitimate sense, refers solely to the actual clouds. To speak of *roky* weather implies thick, foggy weather. The word evidently is connected with *reek* (to steam), but its use, though common enough in this county, is not confined to Norfolk. Again, *thongy,* a thoroughly Norfolk term, describes the oppressive heat which often occurs between two summer showers. *Noah's Ark* is a singular name given to three lines of cloud stretching overhead from the s.w., and supposed to indicate fine weather.

Pulk-hole denotes an open cess-pool. *Waterdelf* is used of an ordinary drainage hole by the roadside, the suffix obviously being from the root *delve,* to dig. *Holl* is a popular word, meaning a wide ditch of water. Possibly it is a contraction of *hollow,* used by Addison to indicate a channel or canal. *Deke*—a bank, and has nothing to do with *ditch* (*cf.* the Dutch *dike*); it is one of the commonest of Norfolk terms, but its origin is obscure.

Bird, in sporting parlance is a partridge. It is interesting to note that *deer* in the same way once meant any animal ("Rats and mice, and such small deer"). However, I don't suggest that *bird* is ever likely to have so exclusive a meaning as *deer* now possesses. What is the force of *together* in "spreed yarselves out together," a direction I have heard given to beaters by a head gamekeeper? And what, too, is the history of the word *duller* in "Howld yew yar *duller*," addressed to a noisy "dorg?"

Wheatsel is a pretty word, meaning "Wheat drilling." Thus, "We've finished wheatsel"—"all our wheat is in." Here the idea is "seed-time," but in *haysel*, for instance, the notion conveyed is that of harvest.

Rig, stitch are both used to describe the space between two double furrows.

Dutfin—a halter. "Fetch a dutfin and show the animal off" is a common expression.

Tussock is an excellent Old English term for a tuft or a sod of grass. It is obsolete so far as the national vocabulary is concerned, and is obsolescent even in remote rural districts.

Heign (heighten)—to raise wages.

Gotch—jug.

Loke—a "blind" lane.

To hank up a gate—to sneck or fasten it.

Fosey—over-ripe.

Lim—to suck. *E.g.*, of a bitch, the pups wil *lim her to deed*—cause her death by sucking.

Tumbler, for tumbrel. Since the word is used of a cart made so as to tip up, "tumbler" is more logical than "tumbrel." Yet "tumbler" is hardly considered respectable.

Muck-crome is a capital word, but is entirely local.

Lit—stain. This occurs in an old saying, "There's not a blot but will *lit*." The word or the proverb is said to be early Danish. I don't know whether anybody has met with it outside this county; at any rate, it is a noteworthy survival.

Fye—to dress corn. Thus, to go *a-fyin* might mean to run wheat through the dressing machine.

An odd vowel change may often be observed. As, for instance,

e for o in *snew* for snow,

i for e in *hin*-bird for hen-bird.

o and even eu for au in *thow* or *thew* for thaw.

o for a in *lond* for land, *sond* for sand, and *grovel*-hole for gravel hole.

I think it is Trench who has pointed out how much richer, at least in rural terms, the English language would be if it adopted freely from its country dialects.   C-H.

(BY THE AUTHOR OF "GILES'S TRIP TO LONDON," &c.)

The first half of my life was passed in the southern parts of Suffolk, and the latter half has been passed in Norfolk. So far as the provincialisms made use of in the two counties are concerned, I think there is not much difference. There is, however, a great contrast in the style of speech. Suffolk speaks in a kind of sing-song; Norfolk in a more broad and sustained tone. There is nothing in Suffolk to answer to the way in which the *a* in certain words is pronounced in Norfolk. Here we say *pauper* and *baaker*, the *a* being drawn out at extraordinary length. This peculiarity does not exist in the sister county. Neither do the people in Suffolk say *rume* for room, or *glumy* for gloomy, as we do here. Neither do they drop the *h*, as the inhabitants of many parts of Norfolk do in some words. A Mid-Norfolk man will say, and even write, for instance, *trow* for throw, *tree* for three, *troat* for throat, and so on. Many of the provincialisms are, as I have said, common to both counties. I will run over a few of them, merely premising that I shall give none which I have not myself heard in the cottages of the peasantry and in the roads and fields.

The terms applied by men and women to each other are interesting. A gi⁻l is called a *mawther*, which, in addressing her, becomes *maw*. "Where have you been, maw?" But she is also called a fine *strappen* mawther. A lad is addressed as "bor," and he is said to be a great *huddren* fellow, or a loose *hulkin'* rascal. If boys or girls are large or jolly they are said to be *swacken*; if they are awkward they are called *gawky*; when out of temper they are *runty*; and when they are half-witted and shiftless they are described as *gatless*. There are many terms to express their doings. They *lollop* or *lummuck* about, or they *sarnter* in the lanes. In the winter time girls and boys *pample* in the mud, and at all times *clamber* up walls or trees. The girls *cop* balls, the boys *cail* stones, and both of them *hull* all sorts of things about. A man will *hull* on his coat, and a women will *hull* on her bonnet. A man will give directions to *hull* a *scuppet* into the barrow and *crowd* it up the hill. The scuppet, of course, is a shovel, and to "crowd" is to drive or push. I have even heard of a man who went into a chemist's shop in North Norfolk and asked for "a punno' o' pills to *hull* a wummen into a sweat." One boy will give another a *clip* o' the head or a *sowse* o' the skull, and I once heard a fellow say he had given another a *sisserara*.

There are a good many terms used inside the cottage which are expressive and peculiar. If you go in when the baby is sleeping, the mother will probably hold up her finger and say, "Don't make a *deen*," which means don't utter a sound. The wick of the candles which at one time were burned in every cottage was called a *snaast*, which the snuffers were used to trim, but if they should not be at hand, the finger and thumb of the father or of one of the boys would do the work. The girl would be sent with a *yotch* to the well, and if she should spill any of the water on the floor, she would be ordered to clean up the *swidge*. If she was disagreeable and put herself into *tantrums*, or begun to *winnock* (*i.e.*, cry), she would perhaps be cut off with only a *hunch* of bread, with maybe an *ingen* (onion), for her dinner. If the mother happened to be ill she would perhaps tell you that she was tired of *sorzles*, the slops which the doctor ordered her, and add that they were nothing but *culch*. Sometimes she would tie a handkerchief around the neck of one of the boys so tightly that he would cry out that he was being *greened*. I used to think about the meaning of this term when I was being greened myself, and thought it might mean that the tight tying would produce a green hue on the skin similar to the colour of a bruise. I expect, however, I was wrong. But even the cottagers had at times their luxuries. Occasionally they would get fried *chitterlings* (the intestines of pigs), or have a dish of *frummety*, which was wheat boiled in milk, or some *guseberry-fule*, which consisted of gooseberries stewed with milk and sugar. Sometimes they would get puddings with *gobs* of fat in them. I remember a song in which the Christmas puddings of the "workhus" were thus celebrated—

>   Great *gobs* of fat they did put in
>   As big as my *tew* thumbs.

But one of the most charming distresses of the housewife was when she was making a batch of bread and happened to " *ming* the miller's eye out." Many a time have I heard this doleful complaint when the good woman has used more water than her flour would carry. She would then proceed to a neighbour's cottage with a basin for a supply sufficient for her needs. Her wise husband would perhaps be *stammed* that she should be so careless, when she might retaliate by asking him how he came to lose one of his *mittens* (gloves with thumb hole but no finger holes), and express the wish that he wasn't such a 'struy for *highlows*, the name given to the rustic's thick lace-up shoes. There are many other domestic terms to which I might refer, but I must pass on.

The fields and the woods are responsible for many provincialisms. What strange names are applied to the living creatures. A snail is a *dodman* or a *hodmandod*, and the boys on capturing one would say, " Hodmandod, hodmandod, pull out your horns," &c. A toad is a *hoppentoad* ; a young frog, such as is found in marshes, is a *fresher*. A boar is a *brawn*, and a rabbit a *bunny*. As for birds, a thrush is a *mavish*, a goldfinch a *King Harry*, and a wood pigeon a *ringdow*, while their nests are *neesen*. By the bye, I may add in a parenthesis that in Suffolk houses are called *housen*, which is doubtless the old Saxon form. There is one little bird—the wren or the tomtit—which was called the *puddenpoke*, from the pudding-like shape of its nest. As for that patient creature which in the Scriptures is called an ass, in London a *moke* or a *neddy*, and in polite circles a donkey, it is universally styled in Norfolk and Suffolk a *dickey*. To have a dickey and cart is a state of affluence for a countryman. A pet lamb is a *cosset* and a guinea fowl is a *comeback* in consequence of the peculiarity of its cry. In the fields the men talk strangely to the horses. When they want them to go to the right they say "*woor-ree*," and when they want them to go to the left they say "*cumhether*." I assume woor-ree means "wear to the right," and cumhether "come hither to the left." But I have heard a man say "Woor-ree cumhether wool ye ?" all in a breath. Any horse or other animal which was quiet and gentle was said to be *toward*. At four o'clock in the afternoon in those days the men in the harvest field had *fourses* or *bever*, which consisted of a "beverage" (which I take to be the derivation of the word) of ale drunk from horns, with harvest cake. What a treat was it then to hear the men "hallo largess." Many a time have I heard them in the distance, and the remembrance even now has in it a touch of romance. The "lord" would ascend a tree and cry aloud "*Hallo lar—hallo lar—hallo lar*," then all the men standing round would add in a low base voice long drawn out *gees*. The effect on a quiet autumn evening just at twilight was remarkable, and I shall never forget it. The remembrance is as a dream of Arcady.

But I must draw these remarks to a close. The expletives, or the mild swearing terms that were adopted by countrymen in my young time, are noteworthy. I refer thus to what things were in the past because, by the influence of the Board schools, everything has been changed, or is rapidly changing. They would *dang* their jackets, or *darn* their buttons, or cry out,

"What the *mendin'* du yew mean?" Of the origin of this last phrase I know nothing. Every reader will recollect that Dickens was puzzled to think of all that might be involved in Mr. Peggotty's great oath, "I'll be *gormed*," which however, is nothing like so common as "*By goms.*" One can see the origin of these terms, as well as why it is said that a thing is *nation* or *tahnation* big or ugly. *Barnt* was a favourite phrase for giving effect to any statement. I knew a woman from Peasenhall who always desired to be barnt everlastingly if she did not speak the truth. If you asked her a question she might say, "Barnt if I know," or she might end a long tale by saying, "There, that's true, barnt if it aint."

In conclusion, it is a common thing to say that a person lives up *hinder* or down *yinder*, and boys and girls are told when they are inquisitive about anything in the household of which they should be kept in ignorance, that it is *lay-over-meddlers.* This is the form given in Moor's "Suffolk Words and Phrases," published in 1823. I am convinced, however, that it should be "La' o' the meddlers, you are the first." This is "Shame on the meddlers, you are the first of them." Mr. Moor's suggestion is ridiculous. He thinks it refers to *layovers or turnovers* which might sometimes be made of medlars instead of apples. By the bye, I was very near forgetting the extraordinary use of the word "together" in both counties. In Suffolk—as I have heard scores of times, and as I have myself doubtless personally exemplified—a friend meeting two or three companions will say in the pleasant sing-song of the place, "Where are yew going, *together?*" "Together" is evidently used as a noun applied to the persons addressed. I think, however, what it really means is this, "Where are you going, you who are here together?" With this suggestion I close my remarks.

It is a mistake to imagine that dialects are everywhere corruptions of the literary language. The real and natural life of language is in its dialects. Even in England the local patois have many forms which are more primitive than the language of Shakespeare, and the richness of their vocabulary surpasses on many points that of the classical writers of any period. — *Max Muller.*

An interesting and useful question in connection with this discussion would turn upon whether it is within the range of possibilities to rescue from the fields and villages a few of the fine, forcible terms which the established language of literature has long since rejected. Until now all efforts to reinstate any of these evicted words have nearly always been in vain. As a matter of fact the word *clever* is almost the only instance of an East Anglian dialectic colloquialism rising into classical English. To facilitate the revival and preservation of the worthy localisms that have fallen into disrepute let us hope will be the result of this rustic symposium.

"What is a *deke*" is a question which, it will be seen, has raised a good deal of disputation. I originally suggested that the word is used in Norfolk to mean a banked up hedgerow rather than a ditch or water-course for draining wet land. Opinion, however, seems equally divided amongst the correspondents. Thus it is tolerably clear that *deke* and *dyke* in different localities of the county are almost interchangeable terms. That curious word usually spelt *sibrits*, but commonly pronounced *sibbits*, is, I believe, generally derived from the Anglo-Saxon *cyb*, meaning "a blood relation." The ubiquitous "plain person" would venture to ask "What have marriage banns to do with blood relations?" Bann is not connected with "bind," but comes from the Saxon word *bannan*, to issue or display a proclamation. Hence the suggestion I heard the other day that *sibbits* is merely a corruption of "exhibits" seems to be a reasonable, as well as an ingenious, explanation. It is true that a majority of the common country colloquialisms can be traced from the recognised language of earlier times, but all the same for that, Norfolk yokels are not to be held altogether innocent of smothering or mutilating the Queen's English. Such words as *backus* (backhouse), *ollust* (always), and *ashup* (ash-heap) are mysteries outside East Anglia.

A characteristic peculiar to rural folk is their habit of keeping up a conversation between themselves, no matter how far they may be off each other. So long as they are within earshot it does not occur to them to approach one another. Labourers (and the old women too) think nothing of gossipping ("having a *mardle*") across a ten-acre field for instance. Depend upon it, the country folk are clinging to their old forms and usages tenaciously enough, but it is to be feared, as Trench has remarked, they cannot resist the moral and material forces which are gradually rendering obsolete all their picturesque phraseology.

Now for one or two additional illustrations of Norfolk speech. Everybody knows that a *pogramite* or *pogrimite* is a contemptuous term for a Dissenter. It would be interesting to know the derivation of this word. Somebody has traced it to Elijah Pogram, the senator in "Martin Chuzzlewit," who was always imagining that the English had a grudge against his free and enlightened country ; as if the word was not widely in use at least a century before the time of Dickens.

A *snasty fule with half a tile off* interpreted, denotes a snarlish fellow weak in the head.

If a woman burnt her finger when cooking *apple-jacks* (apples baked in thin pastry) or *swimmers* (light dumplings), she would put a *hutkin* on it, and in case she was particularly neat and tidy she would *triculate it up like*, so that the injured finger might present a respectable appearance. Anybody with a *game* leg (sore leg) would probably be said to go *himpin* about instead of "limping."

To be in one's *bighes*, a phrase I heard used a day or two ago, seems to imply being in a good mood for the time being.

The list of terms in vogue upon a farm is well-nigh interminable. Besides the large number already given, here are several more:— *Haze*, a term used of corn when, under the influence of sunshine or a breeze, it is drying after a shower of rain. The directions teammen give to their horses vary in different districts. *Cup bear*, meaning come here, *i.e.*, to the left, is of course merely another form of *cum hether* or *cum harley*. *Weesh* or *woosh*, a command to bear to "the right," is actually said to be derived from the French *gauche*, which signifies "the left ! "

Quicks (foul grass) comes from an Anglo-Saxon word with exactly the same meaning.

Skutes—parts of a field of unequal lengths.

The appearance of a *rodger* (a whirlwind on a

small scale) is regarded as a sure sign of fine weather.

It would be easy to give whole columns of quaint superstitions, such as the old charm, "Hick-up snick-up, Three Drops for a Hick-up" or in the condescending injunction of Middle Age to Youth to "eat another yard of plum pudding first," but if I made a serious start in this direction, I should hardly know where to stop. C-H.

Perhaps your versatile contributor "C-H." can tell me something about a phrase with which I am perfectly familiar, and which I believe to be entirely indigenous to Norfolk. "To stand up" is frequently used in the sense of "to shelter," thus, "Let us stand up out of the wet." I am a yokel bred and born myself, and have used, and heard others use, the expression times out of number. So many authorities, however, have expressed themselves entirely ignorant of it that I am tempted to seek further information through your columns. R.W.C.

It was with much interest that I noticed an article in your issue of last Saturday on "Broad Norfolk," since your journal seems the natural medium for placing on record some of those East Anglian terms and phrases which admirers of vigorous expression will not willingly let die. Few people could remain for any length of time in contact with the rural labourers of this district without remarking that they retain the use of many a term—obsolescent, no doubt —but yet indicating in a single word an idea which would require a lengthy sentence to express with equal accuracy. It is generally admitted that all local glossaries at present published possess the defect of including a large number of words which are certainly not limited in their use to the Eastern Counties, as well as the more serious fault of omitting many which as certainly are part of our dialect. An adequate discussion of the subject in your columns would do much to enable our future lexicographer to steer clear of both the rocks which I have indicated.

Among the local terms which immediately occur to me is that singularly complete class of words which indicate the different conditions of corn when lodged by wind or rain. Thus the crop may be said to be "*shackled*," "*knickled*," or "*hovelled*," according to the state in which the storm has left it.

To "*riffle*," *i.e.*, to disturb the surface with a plough; it shares with "*rifle*" the indication of shallow grooves.

One of the first popular expressions which strikes a stranger to Norfolk villages is the frequent use of the phrase, "*It dew fare.*" "*It dew fare wonerful stingy,*" says the rustic, when the wind is in the east.

"*Fourses*" is the afternoon harvest meal, which the labourer takes at 4·30 in the neighbourhood of Norwich.

A man who pottered over his work was said by a farm steward—dead now, poor fellow—to be "*pakin', fussickin', and denesquittin' about,*" which at least sounds a good day's work.

Pickcheesin' has much the same meaning.

I have heard a slow-witted countryman told not to "*stand a garpin' theer, bor, like a duzzy mawkin.*" A stranger to the dialect might wait for more explicit directions.

Many such expressions must occur, especially to those of your readers who reside in districts remote from the larger towns. BOZ.

Your correspondent "C-H.'s" excellent article upon this subject should evoke an interesting correspondence in your columns, particularly among your country readers, many of whom will doubtless be able to add to the list of quaint words and sayings alluded to in the article.

A foreigner visiting this county would think the dialect highly euphonious, particularly if he overheard such an expression as "My master say if I du as I oughter du, I shouldn't du as I du du."

Some of the expressions alluded to by

"C-H." call to mind instances in which similar words have been heard by me, particularly the word "gotch," which recalls the following thoroughly Norfolk sentence, "Polly she tumbled over the trostle (threshold) and broke the gotch." The word "heign" is by no means confined to "wages." I have often heard a bricklayer talk about "heigning a wall." The "o" for "a" is very apparent in the pronunciation of the word "rand" (a marsh bank or wall) which is universally called a "rond" in the broad district. One of the most amusing instances of Norfolk ignorance as well as dialect was one I heard some time ago, when one of the North Norfolk railways was first opened. A Norfolk labourer had never seen a train, but was at work in a field near a bridge over a cutting through which the new line ran. A friend passing said—

"Have you seen a train yet, bor?"

"No, bor, I ha'int."

"Well just yew run up tew the bridge and yew'l see one."

The rustic proceeds to the bridge. Train passes under, whistling. Rustic returns.

Friend—"Well, did you see the train?"

Rustic—"Well, I see suffin, but as sune as that see me that shruck, and rushed into a burra!"

I could give many other instances, but my time and your space will not allow. A NORFOLK DUMPLING.

Referring to the interesting paper on "Provincial Language," I would suggest that the word *duller*, like many other obsolete words, comes to us from the French *douleur* (Latin *dolor*), and is an expression of mental or bodily pain.   N. S.

I think "C.-H.," in his very interesting paper on our Norfolk dialect is in error as to the meaning he gives to the word deke or dike.

He says, "Deke a bank, has nothing to do with ditch." I am inclined to think that it is more nearly allied to ditch than bank. It is a narrow channel of water on marshes, or by the side of roads when there are no hedges. We constantly hear of the deke's mouth, *i.e.*, where the dike joins the river. Then again we hear of Oulton Dike or Deke, Kendal Beke (at the latter in many places there are no banks at all —only reed beds), and boating men will remember many other dikes or dekes. In Holland a dyke or dike is, undoubtedly, a raised bank, but a deke in Norfolk is a water channel, and when a roadway has a deke on both sides it is called a carnser.   C. C.

For the benefit of your correspondent "R. W. C." let me say I have travelled over the greater part of the United Kingdom and have found the expression "to stand up," used in the sense of "to shelter," very general, especially in Kent and Sussex, and, on this side of the Thames, in Essex and Cambridgeshire.
H. B.

As a native, I have read with great interest what has been written on this subject. Allow me to suggest that instead of "Broad" it should be "Pure" Norfolk. In this part of the county we have many expressions which have not yet been catalogued.

Dudder, to shake, or tremble. For example—a drover, a Norfolk man, and two of his neighbours, who were in Essex at the time of the earthquake which occurred a few years ago, were once explaining to a Cockney their experience of the phenomenon. All proceeded pretty well, until one said, " Why, lor, bor, we tree kinder duddered," which, to the knowing young gentleman from the Metropolis, was not very explicit.

Being is a genuine Norfolk word for a home. Mr. Peggotty is anxious "to purwide a bein' for the old mawther."

Mawther. Is not Norfolk pre-eminently distinguished in the use of this word, with its abreviation "mor," which, if not particularly elegant, is, in my opinion, quite as good as "wench" of north country folk any day?

Kinder is in universal use, meaning rather. I suppose it is a corruption of "kind of."

"Norfolk Dumpling" speaks of "*trostle*" for threshold. I never heard it so our way; but "*troshold*" is familiar.

To ask a stranger to hang the kettle on the *hake* and rake up the *hyrers* would puzzle him. Is not hake a pure Flemish word?

To *mung* is used as meaning to knead dough.

Mucky is often used in such a phrase as "mucky action," is one of a disreputable nature.

ew for *oo*. "The man in the mune came down to sune, to ask the way to Norwich," we have known all our lives.

W for V, as wittles (victuals), wexatious, &c.

There is a word in use amongst us which I should much like to have explained. I have asked several, but cannot get a satisfactory definition. When banns of marriage are "asked" we hear of so and so's "sibbits" being read.

Outsiders may laugh at "our language." We are not ashamed of it. Is it not infinitely better than the cockney English of our friends, the Yarmouth Beach singers. We can laugh at the young gentleman as he pensively warbles the

> Hardent wish of 'is art.
> Ho kerry me beck to my oaime ogoain,
> Ho kerry me beck once mower.

Althow this du fare kinder rum to us dumplins, we kinder laarf, bor, when we heer them theer fules, and think our old frind Giles, when he went up to Luunon, wornt any more of a fule than them thoer chaps on Yarmouth Beach. What about 'Arry and 'Arriet, hay, bor? W. H. C.

As one much interested in Norfolk vernacular, may I say a word or two on the subject. I think your correspondent "C. C." is wrong in assuming that "deke" does not mean a bank. It is certainly used for both ditch and bank. As he says a narrow water course through a marsh is a "mashe deke," and a road between two "dekes" is a "carnser" (causeway); but a bank is a "deke" for all that. Witness the expression, "deke's holl." Deke is the bank and "holl" is the ditch (the hollow) adjoining. "Fyeing out a holl" is good Norfolk for cleaning out a ditch. I hope this correspondence will continue, and should occasion serve, I shall be glad on a future occasion to give your readers several good old Norfolk words that I have not yet seen mentioned. "Dannock," a hedger's glove without fingers, is one.

A LOVER OF NORFOLK.

As a north countryman I have been interested in the correspondence on this subject, and I should like to say a word or two. First, I agree with that correspondent who says that "stand up" in the sense of "shelter" is not confined to Norfolk. I have often heard it in other counties.

As to "*dudder*," my acquaintance with Norfolk is not of sufficient length to permit me to express an opinion, but the Lancashire word that has an exactly similar meaning is "dither," as I have heard jelly jokingly termed by Lancashire people "that stuff that dithers."

I hardly think that "*mucky*" is confined to Norfolk. It is often used elsewhere in the sense of dirty.

The word "buskin," and the expression "to put on his parts," strike me as somewhat peculiar to Norfolk. Perhaps some of your correspondents will give their opinion.

As an outsider I can assure you that I do not laugh at your language. As a matter of fact I think it is extremely pretty and euphonious. B. O. P.

I feel little doubt that sibrit, sibrede, or sibberidge (various forms of a provincial appellation of the banns of matrimony) are connected with the old English, or so-called "Anglo-Saxon" word sib, meaning a relation or companion. We find the same stem in the derivatives sibless (without kindred, deserted), sibman (a relative), sibness (relationship), with the old word sibrede, which is synonomous with the last-mentioned. I presume, therefore, that the idea of the banns as preparatory to this new "relationship," gives rise to the name. Or were the "sibrits" for the purpose of bringing to light any kinship or affinity within the prohibited degrees?

E. ROBERTS TUXFORD.

For the edification of neighbour "W. H. C.":—
S·bbits—Siberet—Sybb-rit—Syb rede banna [Prompt. Parv.] When the banns have been published for the third time, the parties are said to have been "out asked."

Hyvers, or *Hovers*, not only means peat, or turf cut for burning, but also a floating reed-bed, where, perhaps, from the nature of the "soil," hovers might be procured. The island in the midst of Scoulton Mere, which might, in parts at any rate, bear this title, is, however, termed the "hearth." Suggested derivation for a "hover" is because it hovers between wind and water! A novice might appreciate the explanation when first experiencing the sensation of the ground for yards around, quivering under his hesitating footsteps.

Holl—a ditch, particularly a dry *one* (Forby)—and so used at the present time, as opposed to

Deke—a wet—that is a water ditch.

We have not yet had the derivation of "Roly poly." Is it from its shape and make a rolled pole?

M. C. H. BIRD.

TIMOTHY TIKKELTOBY TU HIS FRIND MR. GILES.

Well, Bor, an wot d'ye think on't now.
All mauder of stuff they're talkin
Abeout "Broad Norfolk," when they know
No more'n my old mawkin
Which I shuv'd up to frite them bahds
Wot play sich mazin capers,
In fussicken my baanes and paas,
Likewise my arly taters.
If I could nab them knowin chaps,
I'd make 'em keinder dudder,
For laarfin at ower Norfolk tongue,
Why I shud like tu smudder
Sich fules as haint the sense tu know,
They says thay're clever, rawther;
(That's how they say that word, old man)
Yow shud a heer'd my mawther,
She say, yow heer them London chaps
Wet sing on Yarmouth Beach,
Then yow will see and werry sune
Which is the rummest speech.

Yars, or them cockney chaps wot cum
And kick up such a duller,
In murderin that poor letter H.
Yow'l sune see they are fuller
Of cheek than sense, so let 'em laarf.
Doant it seem mazin funny
If we're fules they care tu cum
And glad tu take ower money.
So doant you mind a titty bit
As yow stand theer a garpin,
But let 'em know ower Norfolk tongue
Will stan theer jeers and larfin.
Tell 'em, old man, if we're slow
We arnt at sich a pass,
To brake all rules, and be sich fules
To call our Dickey—Hass.
Ower temper's smuthe, we'll stan theer grins,
An put up with theer crumplin,
We'll hang the biler on the hake
And stick tu NORFOLK DUMPLIN.

W. H. C.

I have read the version of "C.-H." on the word *deke*; he is much more to the point in its use and meaning than "C. C." You will frequently hear the following expression in the country in reference to the word:—"Let's get out of the holl and sit down on the deke." Or when one is jumping over a deke (that is a bank) a caution will be given you—"*warr* (for beware) the *holl* on the other side." The Norfolk fences separating fields are frequently called "dekes." Having had residing experience in Holland, I must say I never heard a dyke is the name given to a "raised bank." There are various dykes named by "C. C." as tributaries to the river, and there are also mill dykes and marsh dykes, which are outlets to drainage mills; but a deke in Norfolk is not necessarily a water channel.

W. S.

Your correspondents have afforded much interest and amusement with their various contributions. The cases cited have been mostly rural words and idioms, many of which one never hears in the city. But there are several words which strike the ear of a stranger as peculiar. The first which misled me for the moment, was " sadly " used in the sense of ill-health, rather than of mental condition. Others were " tempest " for " storm," " coarse " for " rough " weather, and especially the word " muddle " which is a favourite word of Norfolk house-wives, the real English meaning of which is by no means their habit. To a stranger it is very curious to hear methodical industrious people, who seem to have everything in order at the time, describe themselves as " in a muddle."

" B. O. P." cites the word " dudder," which is thoroughly Norfolk. The corresponding word "dither," used in other places, is not a dictionary word, but it is not provincial, for you hear it in the Midlands, as well as in Yorkshire and Lancashire. Its meaning is " slight trembling all over with cold."

I should say " mucky " is essentially a northern provincialism, and one only rarely hears it in Norfolk. In muddy weather it is ever on the people's lips in Lancashire and Yorkshire.

" Here t' be " I never heard save in this county, and perhaps Suffolk. The use of the word " shy " I have never heard explained, but its Norfolk sense is exactly the opposite to its ordinary meaning.

I think " M. C. H. Bird " is right as to the derivation of " roly poly." It appears to stand for " rolled pole," and its diminutive suffixes arose from some maternal desire to give a favourite dish for children, a popular name among them. In this rhyming manner words are better remembered by our juveniles.

J. P. PERKINS.

The correspondence now appearing in your columns is very interesting. Here are a few words I have not yet seen mentioned; and I should like to know if they are confined to Norfolk? They are constantly used amongst us.

To crowd (past crud).—To thrust or push, as " Git the mawther to crowd the barra'. She crud it yisterdaay! "

Deen (for din?)—Strangely enough, this does not mean a loud or continued noise, but the slightest possible sound, as

" Now, yow mussent maak a *deen*, bor ! "
meaning that one must be absolutely quiet.

To imitate.—To attempt, as " I shawn't d'ut, nor yit imitate t' d'ut, bor."
Cooshies.—Sweetmeats. Is this *ever* heard out of Norfolk?
Kindling.—Firewood.
Shortening.—Lard or butter for pastry-making.

J. R. B.

Your correspondents have by no means exhausted the list of Norfolk provincialisms, and have hardly touched upon the many funny terms we use upon our farms and in our country houses. Here are a few :— A " holl " means a ditch, a " deek " means a dyke, a " keeler " means a shallow tub, " kindling " means firewood, a " boiler " means a small tin with a lid, a " dwile " means a house flannel, a " push " means a boil, " over wort " means across, " soshing " means askew, " sidus " means a sloping, " cop " means to throw, " hain " means to rise (*vide* the Rev. W. Hudson's " Norwich Chronicles.")

Then there are no end of miscalled words. For instance, a tumbrel is called a " tumbler," a bin is called a " bing," a shovel is called a " shuloe," a headland is called a " hidlond," bran is called " brun," a marsh is called a " mash," and curiously enough we still talk of going down to " mash," and giving a horse a " brun marsh."

The language we address to our cart horses would puzzle the carters of other counties. When a horse is wanted to go to the right we say " woosh," to the left " cum harley." When he is is stop we halloo " way." A team of horses is called a " teamer," and the carter a " teamerman."

I once cautioned an ostler to be careful how he took out my mare, whereupon he patted her on the neck and said " She fare toward like tho." A London friend I was driving was sorely puzzled at the remark, and I had to translate it—" Notwithstanding what you say the mare appears to be quiet and gentle." The same gentleman was also surprised to hear a labourer at an agricultural show remark, upon looking at a sleek black pig, that it put it put him " mazen in mind of a moll," which we need not say meant that the pig very much resembled a mole. I can remember, when a child, hearing some old folk use the word " Frenched " (violent anger), and the "ham" with which many places ended was always "gim," as "Gimmingim," but they are extinct, as also "silly bold" for impudence; but "dicky," "dodman," and other rustic names still survive. Many of your readers may remember the picture of two Norfolk boys in *Punch* and one exclaiming, "Hinder come a dow," which had to be rendered into the Queen's English thus, "In the distance a wood pigeon is coming." The number of old Norfolk phrases and miscalled words are still almost endless, but the Board schools will possibly eradicate most of them in the next generation.

A NORFOLK FARMER.

Will one of your philological correspondents give the origin and *ideal* meaning of the teamman's (Norfolk for "teamster," never heard "teamster" used) "hait" and "woosh"? I don't suppose these are exclusively Norfolk words, but I know they are indispensable to the Norfolk ploughman, and with "*wae*" are among the best understood by our farm horses.

If I say "*hait*" my horse turns to the left, "*woosh*" and he turns to the right. Why? and whence come these words?

I have my theory, but wish for a scholar's opinion.

CHAS. BUSSEY.

I think your correspondent "W. H. C." will find that the use of the vowel "*u*" for "*o*" is restricted to East Norfolk. One never hears of "mune," "spune," and "butes" in West Norfolk. I append a few more Norfolkisms which I have not at present seen mentioned:—The heron is very often called a "*harnser*," whilst the wood pigeon is a "*dow*," as illustrated in the thoroughly Norfolk sentence of "Hie into the holl, bor! hinder cum a dow."

You may perhaps also hear a farm steward threaten a sheep-boy with a "*clink*" or a "*clout*" of the head if he does not properly attend to his "yows" (ewes).

The word "*romant*" takes the place of the verb "imagine." "*Sharm*" is to shout; "*starmed*" means amazed; and "*hull*" and "*cop*" both mean to throw.

I think that although there is something to be said on both sides with regard to the word "*deke*," meaning either "bank" or "ditch," in sound it most approaches the latter, and in this district certainly is always used for "ditch." Fen men also would understand "*deke*" to be a channel of water, and in Lincolnshire their "doike" is the same.

WEST NORFOLK.

There are one or two phrases which have been omitted, although doubtless they are well known to your correspondents, viz.:—"That dew rain a *suffin*." "I gin her a *funny mobbin*." "There ain't *enow*" (for enough). "He's *sammucking alonger* his mawther" (strolling aimlessly). Upon inquiring after a person's health, one is often told that "He's *nicely* thank ye." When a horse is fresh he is said to be "*gaily*."

TEW CHAPS.

The interesting letters appearing in your columns anent words and phrases peculiar to Norfolk and Suffolk have not yet exhausted the list, for I do not recollect seeing any mention of the following:—

"A *good tidy* lot," a great many; "all mander of what," a *very* miscellaneous collection of articles, notably such as might come out of a boy's pocket; *hulvers*, for holly bushes; *gaffer*, an old man; and *doke*, a hole, such as might be made by pressing the hand into a featherbed.

ONE INTERESTED.

Not Norfolk born, I notice many forms of expression unfamiliar, though whether or not peculiar to Norfolk, I cannot say. The intonation is certainly peculiar, and the Norfolk man is undoubtedly a wit. He nearly always takes pains both to nod his head in the general direction of anything or place he may be referring to, and also to express himself somewhat in the way of parable. For example, a man said to me of one in feeble health, "He won't carry old bones." Doubtless many of their forms of expression are archaisms, and quite as correct as her Majesty's Inspector's pattern English, such as *lief* and *enow*.

The Norfolk man is essentially cautious, and for him to say it is *moderate* means not good, and that there were *several* means a great many. Surely it is sufficient explanation of *mucky* that manure is muck. Perpetually he speaks of *imitating* to do, that is attempting or professing. He always *lays* instead of lying; a horse *himps*, not limps; the soil should be *moultry*; a *mess* is a certain quantity; a pool is a *swish* of water; supports his wall with *a spore* not a shore; if better, he is *gettin' on the round*, he *sets* not sows his seeds; has a *hasel* and a *barksel*; and in the littər a pitman. If frightened he is only astonished: he *rightsides* his boy or his dog; things may be *illconvenient*; he may have a *rare* cold, rare being superlative in any direction; the east wind is *stingey*, the windows may *rattick*, or the fire *squinder*. Though the present tense is never favoured with its final "s," yet it always is with a strange perversion:—"It *don't* matters," and "it *don't* seems to." He knows no distinction in *Furrin* parts; so to "go to Jericho" is the same as to "go to Bungay."

"Du yu let them chickens out, and she'll *troll* 'em to dead," was a piece of advice once tendered to me in favour of keeping the old hen in a coop. One with a "screw loose" is *shanny, not quite rocked*, or *won't get further than Wednesday*. Curious and ingenious, and probably grammatically defensible, is the hypothetical use of the word *do*, which is commonly observable, as for example in such a sentence as this —"He don't fare to be a-comin," *do* that don't matters," where 'do' supposes the fact that "He do fare to be a-comin'" Such points I have commonly observed when such sentiments would be expressed "So fashion."   R. G. W. TUCKER.

On coming from church yesterday (Sunday), I heard a holly bush called a *Christmas tree*; that it was a slow *thow*; that the frost *fare to forgive*; and later on, that the old yows *mauled* their turnips better. And this morning, as a sort of mild swearing, "*Gorn sim your body, bor!*"
   A NORFOLK FARMER.

For the "edification" of "W. H. C." and Mr. Bird and all others whom it may concern, probably a very numerous class, I have looked up the following:—Nathan Bailey's Dictionary, 1722, says:— *Sib* (Saxon) kindred—*Sib'd*, a-kin, as no sole sib'd— nothing a-kin, North Country ; and *Sibbered* and *Sibberedge* from *Sybbe* (Saxon) kindred—The banns of matrimony, *Suff.*

Readers also of Sir Walter Scott may perhaps remember the following passage in the *Antiquary*:— " By the religion of our Holy Church they are ower *sib* together. But I expect nothing but that both will become heretics as well as disobedient reprobates, that was her addition to that argument—and then, as the fiend is ever ower busy with brains like mine, that are subtle beyond their use and station, I was unhappily permitted to add, ' But they might be brought to think themselve sae *sib*, as no Christian law will permit their wedlock.' "—" Waverley Novels," 1854, vol. 6, page 157.

But Nall in his "Dialect and Provincialism of East Anglia" perhaps gives the fullest description of the word. He says it is one of Sir Thomas Browne's words, that it occurs in an entry of the old Assembly books of the Yarmouth Corporation during the reign of Charles I., where the parson is entreated in consequence of the increase of poverty to forbear to take any banns, ask any *cybredds*, or marry any poor person either with or without license. Nall's work is a very excellent one, and contains most of the words which your correspondents have sent you, and those who wish for further information about *sibbits* would do well to consult it, as also Bailey.   JOHN L. CLEMENCE.

Permit me to submit to your notice a few more specimens of the above.

Tissicken, irritation, irritating. I have a " tissicken " in my throat, a tissicken cough. [*Phthisicking*.]

Kane, water at low tide between the outer sand bank and the beach. " I shall bathe in the kane."

Pawk, to search. Persons searching for anything cast upon the beach by the waves are locally known as " pawkers." What are you " pawking " after.

Swop, to fall heavily. " I fell down ' swop.' "

Say, to weigh down.

Closes, fields with a footpath through them.

Pightle, a small field.
Back Stalk, the back of a low hearth.
T'year or *To year,* "Have you dug any potatoes ' to year'" is a very common expression.
Par Yard, cows or bullocks' yard.
Hen's Polly, a hens' roost.
Dingle, make haste and don't "dingle."
Larrup, a small quantity. " Well! there's a larrup to bring."
W. H. C.

If there is yet space in your columns on this subject permit me to add some words and peculiarities at present, I believe, unnoticed by your various correspondents.

Squezen'd, overcome by heat or nearly suffocated. *Quackled,* having one's breath momentarily taken away. *Golder,* to laugh in defiance. *Tupe,* to drink a quantity at one draught. *Trape,* to trail (as a dress upon the ground). *Jowl,* to peck at (as birds do at any hard substance). *Splarr,* to spread or sprawl. *T'do,* a fuss. *Gay,* a picture of any kind. *Fawny,* a ring. *Fang,* to clutch. *Pakenose,* an inquisitive person. *Lig,* a heavy load or burden. *Frowy* (also *Fysty*), spoken of food when going bad or mouldy. *Shug* (also *Shig*), shake. *Run,* to leak or become liquid. *Comforter,* a scarf or muffler. *Dingle,* to travel slowly. *Refuge,* to put in a place of shelter (spoken in reference to cattle). *Out abroad,* outside the house.

There is also a peculiar use of such words as *Crumb, Duty, Good, Do* and *Don't, Time,* and *Without,* as the following examples will show :—

"Cut me a *crumb* o' beef." "What's his *duty* (occupation) ?" "Hull it out abroad; that's no more *good* (no further use)." "You aru't old enough *du* (or) you might a tried." "Shet that gaate, bor, *don't* (if not) yar old sow'll girrout." "Wait outside *time* (while or during the time) I'm gone in." "Don't do it *without* (unless) you're sure about it."

I may say I can personally vouch for all I have written.
FRED. R. FORSTER.

The correspondence on the above subject is proving most interesting, but, for my own part, I should like to see something more stated as to the source of these words and terms. Here are a few others that I have not yet seen mentioned:—"Dowshie," a large hoe used for scraping roads; "Piece," instead of field; "scald," the highest part of a hilly field; "rattiker" a footbridge; "rattick," to shake or knock about; "grup," for ditch or dyke; and "beck," generally supposed to be obsolete, is still used in Norfolk to denote a small running stream. "Colder" is a word that has two meanings; in the county it is understood to mean the husks of wheat or chaff of some kind, while in the city bricks' ends and other rubbish from old buildings is what is meant. The term, "lay-over-meddlers," used in the article of this morning, is rather different from what I have myself heard. When too inquisitive as to certain things I have been informed they were "lar-o'-for-meddlers, and you are the first." "Kub ba-hoult" is used every day by the Norfolk teamman, but I could never quite make out its meaning.

An Irishman would be known by his "brogue" in any part of the world, but we do not so often hear of a Norfolk man being thus recognised, therefore the following may be interesting:—A young man, a native of Norwich, was at work in Canada. Whilst walking along a road one cold morning he was accosted by a stranger with "Sharp morning, this!" He at once replied in true Norfolk style, "Ah, *bor*, you're right." The stranger stopped, looked sharply at him, and said, "What part of the world do you come from?" The young man was somewhat surprised, but said he came from England. The stranger did not seem satisfied with this, but asked for the particular part of England, and gave, as his reason for being so inquisitive, that he had never heard the word *bor* used outside a certain district. The young man at once gave his address, and then his name, whereupon the stranger grasped his hand, and said, "That's the masterbit; I used to live next door to yer father, and I ha' nussed you many a time when you wor a nipper." JOSKIN.

It is most useful to preserve the fast-vanishing relics of old country dialects, and, therefore, all the more necessary to guard against recording as local, words which are widely current. May I give a few instances from the interesting article on "Broad Norfolk" by the author of "Giles's Trip to London" in your issue of the 9th instant?

Bunny—For rabbit, is, I believe, used throughout England, certainly in all the Southern counties. Chitterlings—This word is used in London and the south generally. Clamber—Is universal. Dang and Darn—Are of daily, nearly hourly, used in Surrey and Sussex. Gawky—May be heard all over England. Hoppen toad—Surely is merely hopping toad. Hulkin and strappen—Anywhere in these isles one may hear of hulking lads and strapping lasses. Tantrums—Are not peculiar to East Anglia in word or fact.

Neither the word nor the bird *mavis* is peculiar to East Anglia, as all may know who have heard the pretty Scotch song in which occurs the couplet—

"I heard the mavis singing
Her love song to the morn."

The word is in Chaucer, and its origin is interesting. In early Latin texts this poetic bird was termed *malvitius*, from *malum*, bad, and *vitis*, a vine, it being very harmful to the vines. In Germany it bears a name of similar meaning. The transition from *malvitius* to mavis is of course easy.

Of one local word I should be very glad to know the proper meaning and derivation—the word *corder*. The Rev. G. S. Barrett asked for information as to this in January last year, but none seems to have appeared. The word may be seen on new notice boards on land about Catton. The words *olf*, a bull-finch, *doke*, a trench, and *duzzy*, strange or devilish, are of some interest.

I am afraid to encroach too much on your space, but perhaps you will permit me to say that George Borrow (whose memory Norfolk would do well to cherish more warmly) used many localisms in his works. Did he not say that it is "in Norfolk where the people eat the best dumplings in the world, and speak the best English?" Borrow frequently gives the *sele of the day*, sometimes insists on *being his share* in paying for the good ale his soul loved, and says *Go you there, see you here*, and so on. He uses the following words, hastily selected, which are, I believe, genuine East Anglian, viz.:—Crome, driftway, dwile, freshets (perhaps misprint for freshers), highlows, shack, staithe, and tumbril. I am not sure whether *spuffling* is a practice peculiar to East Anglia. The word dodman, or hodmandod, is found in old plays, and occurs in Christopher Anstey's *New Bath Guide* :—

So they hoisted her down just as safe and as well,
And as snug as a hodmandod rides in his shell.

The vigour of English literature owes a good deal to dialects, and the English language is a grand mosaic. As an old lexicographer says, " beautified and enriched out of other tongues, partly by enfranchising and indenizening foreign words; partly by implanting new ones with artful composition, our tongue is as copious, pithy, and significative as any other in Europe."

I, for one, hold that in the wide world you may search in vain for so noble a mother tongue as is ours, welded and wrought in the sinewy strength of a race builded and compounded of the best blood the earth has ever borne.

If this be so, Mr. Editor, you cannot regret that your columns have been opened to discuss the history and the vitality of one strand in the glorious web and woof. " HET VARKE."

I have been much interested in the letters and articles appearing in your paper with reference to the Norfolk dialect. Before you bring the closure to bear, I should like to have a word or two on the subject.

In the first place I would point out to the author of "Giles's Trip" that the word *housen* is not peculiar to Suffolk as it is in frequent use in Norfolk. The Saxon form of denoting the plural number is still extant in such words as "oxen" and "children." The Rev. J. P. Perkins is also wrong in supposing that the word *mucky* is not common in this county. Presumably he has never heard of "muck spreeding" or known of a man being called a "mucky slink," a term of reproach, which is often used. This brings to my mind other words used to denote some mental failing in the individual, such as *duzzy fule, silly chump, shanny brain,* and *cranky*. The latter word, no doubt, is derived from "crank," but I fail to see why it should be used in the sense commonly understood. In visiting a small farmhouse you enter over the *troshold* and are invited by the good lady into her *keepin rume*, a name peculiar, I think, to this county, given to the room most generally used by the family, the " parlour " being only u-ed on high days and holidays. I have also heard the expression used even in Norwich. There is one charge that cannot be brought against the local dialect, and that is the wrong use of the aspirate. Norfolk people know how to sound their " H's." VERDANT GREEN.

I have been greatly interested by the letters in your paper on "Broad Norfolk." As a native of East Norfolk, in which part the broadest of the broad is used, I recognise nearly all the words as being used when I was a boy in the district for many miles round Stalham. To a Londoner the Norfolkese was an unknown language, and I have frequently had occasion to act as interpreter between my London friends and some of the older natives (the i very long please).

There appears a doubt as to the use of the word *deke*, as to whether it is applied to an earth bank or a narrow watercourse. In East Norfolk it certainly is used in both senses thus : " My ol l dickey clambered over the *deke* into Cubit's pightle last night, and jampt his mangels about a rummen ;" or, " My little mawther Sukey (pronounced Suker) hulled my velvet frock (velveteen sleeved waistcoat) into Riches's *deke* last night : lor, bor, that wor in sum mess of a pickle when I switched it out with the muck rake I was a-usin." Usually in my part they prefix the *liquid deke* with the word " water," and speak of it as a *water deke*.

In my book " The Land of the Broads," on pp. 249-254, I give a list of about 130 obsolete words, sufficient as I thought at the time, for the purpose of calling the general readers' attention to our fast disappearing Norfolkese, but I fancy with a little thought I could bring the total up to 250. My book, after going through three editions, is now out of print, but doubtless a copy is to be seen in the Norwich Free Library.(If not I shall have pleasure in presenting a copy on hearing from the secretary).

While on the subject of Norfolk peculiarities, may I mention the curious custom (one thing leading to another) of nearly every man and boy in East Norfolk being known by a "nickname." This custom appertains so far in Yarmouth, among the fishermen, that very few of a crew are ever known by their real names. Some of the names are given because of personal peculiarities, while others are perfectly enigmatical in their reference to the individual indicated. Here are half-a-dozen I think of as I write. *Two-Skull* (Thompson), *Lightskin* (Hewett), *Punks* (Wiseman), *Rollaboy* (Mason), *Phantom* (Cubitt), *Whale* (Williams), &c., all of them known to me as a boy. If you go aboard a Yarmouth lugger to seek a certain man, it is quite necessary that you should first know his cognomen, or one stands a very poor chance of finding one's quest. ERNEST R. SUFFLING.

Shortly, from the information given by your various correspondents, it will not be difficult to collect materials for the basis of a respectable glossary of Norfolk words, corruptions, and queer phrases. I think, however, that we have not yet heard if a person apes superior speech he *frame*, or that if we tell him so he is likely to turn *snasty*, and, if provoked too far, might give us a *ding i' the chaps*, and *maak no bones about it nahther*. A *rare piece of wurrk* is a disturbance or quarrel, and a juvenile old lady is a *kidgy old wumman* If we go in search of an article we *hyke it up*, and in *fardenter, hayper, panner, shillinter*, the *er* or *ter* is equivalent to "worth." To *jamb* on is to tread upon. I heard a genuine Norfolkman say once to a lad who had had the misfortune to graze his nasal organ, *Warra yow done t' yar nooze bor? Blundered down an jamped on 't?* J. R. B.

Your correspondent "West Norfolk" points out that the use of the vowel "u" for "o" is restricted to East Norfolk and the author of "Giles's Trip" remarks upon the different style of speech and pronunciation here and in South Suffolk. The same thoughts struck me on reading the earlier contributions on the above subject. In fact, I said "this is *broad* Norfolk indeed," most of the provincialisms quoted being now at any rate peculiar to the "broad" district.

I am sorry to say that *hallowing larges* (the double
"s" was never pronounced) is a thing of the past,
although the "haller holder or holger boys" at haysel
and harvest are as vociferous as ever. With respect to
the *dike* and *deke* controversy, I have heard a raised
bank with a ditch on each side of it spoken of as a
fosse several times within the past four years. The
only word in which the letter "h" is added wrong-
fully to my knowledge is in *hilder*, meaning the elder
tree (Sambucus niger).

Pogramite. Is this a corruption of Pilgrim and Progress, a pogramite having in early days to make a
long pilgrimage to his meeting-house? I knew an old
lady in Essex who used to lock up her cottage and
walk seven miles every Sabbath to meeting. When
accompanying two men rabbiting some twenty years
ago, a ferret "laid up;" one man told the other to
put a second ferret in, whilst doing so he observed
"go in Pilgrim and search out Progress." It had
been a dull morning, when at length the sun began to
break out the same man saluted him thus, "here come
little Phœbe."

Rodger's blast, alias *Sir Roger*, may be a corruption
of Sirocco, as rattick is of rickety.

A man who *himps*, and especially if he uses a crutch,
I called a *hop and go one*, or a *dot and go one*, the dot
being the mark made on the ground by his crutch. I
have never heard "kane" used as mentioned by
"W. H. C.," a small lake left by the receding tide
being usually termed a "low." Has the term "to sag"
any connection with the Greek *sagéne?* A net makes
a bag where it "sags."

Wake.—An open piece of water when the rest of the
Broad is "laid," has its Norwegian equivalent
"wak."

When I used to ask what a parcel contained, and it
was thought unnecessary for me to know, I used to be
told "*Rare o's for medlers, a box o' the ears for in-
quirers.*"

Why should "God bless yer" be said to a person
when sneezing?

One need not go abroad to get to "furrin parts."
The "Sheers" were far enough removed from Broadland until "Puffin Billy" opened up the district.

I once, as a "draw," asked a man what he thought
of the Education Act, and so many cubic feet of air
being required for every child, &c., a new

schoolroom being in course of erection near by. "Well," he said, "yow can get 100 cubic foot o' air into a werry small space, yer know." When told that one of a pair of soles which he offered for sale did not match in size, he answered, "Well, now yow cum to mention it, dale me if I dew think they fare to corroborate." Another old salt observed the preparations for trying the new life-saving rocket apparatus in majestic silence; when the rocket was fixed he drew near, and eyeing it suspiciously for a moment or two, took off his sou' wester, scratched his head, and thus soliloquised, "I think I'll give that there rume," meanwhile retreating to a respectful distance. That man had braved an Arctic winter, but here on his own native sands thought discretion the better part of valour. I have modified his language just a trifle!
M. C. H. BIRD.

While thanking you for inserting my yesterday's letter, I should like to supplement it by adding a few more phrases that have since occurred to me. Bread, when coming from the oven underdone is described as *slackbaked*. If a person denies the statement of another he is denounced for *tellin' me to my hid 'twas a story*. A foremost person in some assembly is reckoned a "*kinder hid-sc-rag*." If an unusual number of people are met together there is bound to be, on first seeing them, *suffin' the matter*. One who has a well-supplied table at meals is said to "*live like old Pamp*." Should the fumes from burning garden refuse assail the nasal organ there is "*a quickfire somewhere*." When a person has little to do and is asked to go somewhere with a message, &c., he is informed *it will be all honest your time*. To "*rip and slash about*" is to drive furiously. To seem insincere and smooth tongued is to *keep a carneyin'*. Taking big strides when walking is to *lamper along*. Goods being sent abroad are *goin' forrin'*. To hasten work unusually in preparation for something is to *lay forrard*. I do not know whether this final example is peculiar to Norfolk, but it is very prevalent hereabouts. For instance, after two or more persons have been engaged in a lengthy argument, one of them caps the whole thing by ejaculating that encouraging phrase, *Well, there 'tis!* Beyond this statement in a case of that kind it seems (to me) impossible to go!
FRED. R. FORSTER.

All interested in the preservation and record of our Norfolk dialect must feel greatly obliged to you for the very entertaining and valuable help you are now according the subject. As I have had some opportunity—in various parts of Norfolk—of noticing the many peculiarities of our phraseology and provincialisms, may I add a few to the list of words fast becoming obsolete in our county?

As to *deke*, might I suggest that when used for *dyke* or *holl* the derivation comes from the Anglo-Saxon *dic*, connected with the German *teich*—a pond; and when used as synonymous with bank, it comes from the Dutch *dijk*, or dike, the "i" having the usual "e" sound peculiar to Norfolk.

Now for a few Norfolkisms which I have not yet noticed in your paper. Amongst verbs we have *shruck* for shrieked; *scriggle*, to turn about worm-like; *golder*, to laugh noisily; to *howe*, for to hoe; *thowt*, past tense of think.

Amongst food names everyone says *rows and milches* for roes and milts; the baked skin of pork is *crackley* or *skruzzle*; long suet puddings are *donkey-legs*; pork cheese is *swared*; and the cartilege in beef is *pax-wax*.

The nicknames of animals are often very pretty; winkles become *pinpatches*; ladybirds are *bish-q-barney bees*; and the stickleback is a *stannicle*. A little animal of the dormouse kind I used to hear called a *ranny*. A common expression for a bad boy is an *aainter* or *nointer*; while one who is inured to hardships is a *hard-woolled-un*.

A number of our provincialisms are of course onomatopoetic in character, as instance *krinkle*, *slammakin*, *swack*, and the terms for crying, such as *slobber* and *blare*. Norfolkers, as well as other people, have a habit of transposing consonants, as in *waps* for wasp, *ax* for ask, &c. One wonders why a lad who "truants," your yokel would say—is said to *play the Charley*, or *play Sammy*. It is easier to see why the boy, if in hiding, is told to keep *squat*, or close and quiet; and doubtless he'd be *all o' a molt*, for fear of getting *summit of a hiding* were he found in hiding by his *feyther*.

A woman's ejaculation is often "Sakes aliye," or "sars o' mine." I see one of your correspondent's says a wash tub is a *kecler*, but is it not oftener called a *killer*. What is a *swap-tub*?

Some of your readers may not know that Bartlett

in his "Dictionary of Americanisms" says, "Those parts of Great Britain which have contributed most to our provincialisms are the Counties of Norfolk and Suffolk, and the Scottish Borders." And Elwyn, in his "Glossary of Supposed Americanisms," thinks one would find more true Saxon and Anglian words in the New England States than even in England itself. It would be a splendid thing were someone with the time and ability to revise and supplement our local works on East Anglian dialects, of which even the leading works, like the Rev. Rob. Forby's "East Anglian Glossary," Major Moor's "Suffolk Words," and Nall's "Dialects and Provincialisms of East Anglia," are very imperfect. A very amusing specimen of Norfolk language is "The Song of Solomon," written by the Rev. E. Gillett (of Runham) for Prince Louis Bonaparte's collection of English dialects. The 10th verse of chapter vi. reads "Who's she as star out as the mornen, feer as the mune, shear as the sun, and frightful as a army wi banders." W. S. BARKER.

In view of the very interesting correspondence on this subject, perhaps some of your readers may be glad to know of a local variation of usage in two of the words which have been much discussed, viz., *dike* and *deke*, or *deek*.

Here in Lynn and the neighbourhood the word *dyke* is invariably used for a watercourse or drain, and the last few weeks everybody has been skating on the *dykes*.

In my native village, less than twenty miles from here (in the neighbourhood of Hunstanton) the word "deek" was always used to signify a *hedge bank*, the waterway being a *ditch*, or more commonly a "*grup*." This was the case from twenty to thirty years ago, and for aught I know the same usage prevails now. "Now then, come down orfe that there *deek* together," would be a very common salutation to us youngsters if we got up to look over a hedge, &c.

This would appear to be a corruption of the Dutch use of the word "*dyke*" for bank, which, notwithstanding what one of your correspondents seems to imply, has been immortalised in the great historic scene of the cutting of the dykes by William of Orange to drown out the Spanish armies. F. W. B.

In the unique list of Norfolk terms you are giving, the following I think have not been mentioned: *swiving* I remember being used when a "yunker" to mean mowing with a reap-hook. The words *hample* and *wimple trees* are often used of the poles connecting horse traces with farm harrows or the like. We call bullfinches *bloodulfs*, and chaffinches *spinks* about here. If our wives make us heavy dumplings we complain that they are *mastrous sumpy*. But we don't often have to find fault with them. Bullock-tenders always call their baskets *skeps*. S.

Under your heading "Broad Norfolk" you have started a most amusing subject of discussion. I have been waiting to see what would be said about the common and very curious use of what has come to be an adverb or adverbial particle, the word *do*, pronounced, of course, "dew." Two of your correspondents this morning, Messrs. Tucker and Forster, are on the right scent, the latter treating it as equivalent to "or," the former rightly explaining it as short for "if you do." This is simple enough, after negative propositions, such as prohibitions, *e.g.*, "Don't you do that again, *dew* I'll give you a hiding." But I have constantly heard it used after positive sentences, with the meaning, "If I or you don't or didn't." A good instance I remember when I was out shooting. Some birds having lighted in a bare clover field, and it being desirable to drive them back to turnips, the keeper peeps incautiously over the fence and the birds go wrong. "Peter," I say, "why did you show yourself? Didn't you see the birds?" Peter replies, "Well, sir, I see somethin' in the olland, but I thought it was muck, *dew* I'd a bopped." That is, if he had not thought so he would have ducked his head. (*Bopped*—bobbed.) Mr. Forster seems to think *don't* would be used in such cases where "if not" is required. But *do* is employed in both collocations, and may be said generally to be equivalent to "under changed conditions and circumstances"—a brief and handy substitute.

Olland in the above dialogue is old land where the clover has been twice mown or fed off, and so effete, ready to be ploughed up for wheat. It is more commonly called *layer* or *lay*, which I take to be the same word as *lea*.

Let me make a remark or two on other words mentioned in your correspondence this morning. A *gay* is not only a bright picture, but a bright flower. "Can't you mow the aftermath in the churchyard before Sunday?" "Not time enough, sir, but I'll cut off they *gays*," meaning conspicuous hemlock heads, dandelions, &c., growing on the fence.

Froschy is pure Anglo-Saxon, frosch being a frog in German.

Bor again may be the German *baur*, which also survives in *boor*. But some take it to be *neighbour* beheaded.

Snasty I take to be a sort of unconscious *crasis*, or combination of *snarling* or *sneering* and *nasty*. Compare the phrase in Article XVII., "wretchlessness of unclean living," where I have always thought the compilers of that document had "wretched recklessness" in their minds and slurred the two words together.

Let me add to Mr. Tucker's illustrations of a Norfolk man's caution when you offer him something distinctly good—he never says he will be glad to accept it. "Will you come up to the house to supper tonight?" "Well, sir, I d*o*n't mind."

C-H's account of *skute* is hardly complete. It is an acute-angled triangle. "Lynn Scute" is a well known whin covert so shaped. There is a verbal form "That there piece go *skuting* away"—meaning to a point.

I hope somebody will give us the etymology of *wheesh*, used to turn a horse to the right. It cannot surely be *gauche*.   A. G. D.

I am glad to find the "Broad" Norfolk correspondence has "*caught on*" so well and is still flourishing. The same idea has struck me that has occurred to your correspondent, "M. C. H. Bird," viz., that Broad Norfolk may mean the dialect of the "Broad" districts, and this idea is strengthened by your correspondent from Swaffham who repudiates the use of u for oo, as in the words "*bute*," "*spune*," "*sune*," "*nune*," &c., in the West Norfolk district. It is certainly a most marked attribute of the Broad district dialect.

Surely, sir, some of your correspondents must have a very imperfect sense of sound. I know very well the difficulty of phonetic writing, and of conveying sound by letters, but surely it is a little too much when we find the common teamman's words, "*kep haa*" (come hither), and *woosh*, made into "*cum harley*" and "*worree*," sounds which I venture to say were never heard in this part of Norfolk.

Mr. Tucker gives us a "*swish*" of water. I think the phrase ought to be "swidge."

I append two or three examples which I have not yet observed.

Tolc, to entice. The last time I heard this was in this wise. I lent a man a young dog for snipe shooting. He got on very well till he had to cross a river. He tried to *tolc* the dog into the boat, but he declined to be tolced, and came off home.

Another good old word which will probably soon become extinct is *goaf*, corn stacked in a barn. "Git on to the *goaf*, bor, and hull down some 'shoves.'"

Plancher or *planchard*, a chamber floor, is still frequent, and till within the last forty years was commonly used by persons of some education. In "Webster" it is given as an obsolete word, meaning, 1st, a floor, and 2nd, a plank, from which I infer it was used by our forbears to designate the *wooden* chamber floor in contradistinction to the *brick* floor of the lower room.

Turn to, in the sense of to set about a job, is a frequent expression in this part.

I fear I have already trespassed too far, so must reserve any further remarks for a future occasion.

OLD NORFOLK.

To your very interesting list of words may I add that many years ago I heard more than once the word *mort*, used for illness—*i.e.*, "I am very *mort* to-day?"

Has the strange word been given of *spoat*, for short-grained wood?

I think *deke* certainly means a hedge bank about here, but then there are no water ditches.

I may add that though many strange words are in constant use about here (the Cromer district), yet it is easy to know any countryman from inland by his far stronger accent.

N. NORFOLK.

I have been much amused by the letters and articles which have appeared in your paper on the above. There is one word (there may be many) which I have not seen; that word is *sunkets* or *sunketing*. It is applied in this way. Say a man has been on the fuddle or boose for a week; he naturally feels rather shaky, and in order to get himself back to his normal state he takes all sorts of niceties i.e., *sunkets*; or he is said to be *sunketting* himself. It is not peculiar to Norfolk, as I have heard it in Suffolk.

As to the Norfolk dialect being recognised in far off climes, I can fully bear out your correspondent, "Joskin." Some years ago I was an officer on a barque lying in Valparaiso Bay. One day I took the ship's gig and four hands to fetch the captain, who had gone on a visit to another ship. On approaching it I gave the order for the men to lay in their oars. A man who was leaning over the rail or bulwark immediately called out, "Come on, bor, you're a *towney* of mine; you're Norfolk." When we got into conversation I found he was like me—a Yarmouth man. S. T. CLARKE.

I have read with considerable interest the "Broad Norfolk" correspondence, and offer a few more words of that language. *Lock*, a bunch; *whasking*, a beating; *rum*, funny; *spoult*, brittle; *gavvel*, a bundle of hay ready for cutting; *douse-a-bit*, how-so-be-it; *lork-a-masser*, Lord have mercy; *snob*, shoemaker; *nip along*, run fast; a frosty day is called *a good steward*; *hobby*, pony; *shornt*. shall not; *gainer*, handy. W. L.

With this, my "third time of asking" your permission to insert some further provincialisms, I close the list so far as I am concerned, at the same time thanking you for the indulgence shown me.

To be brief *the thing in't* is this here:—*A sploddin'* all in the *sluss* and not lookin' what he was *arter*, that there little *brudler* tumbled down and made his clothes *in a rare pass*, for his coat wi' the *daarrt* dried on to't fare as tho' t'would *stan' aline o' muck*. *Wot the plague* d'yow ail, bor? Well, mor, I don't feel *up to a sight.* Don't ye? I noticed *yesterdaay, thinks I*, he *rarely well* keep a *pinglin'* over and *champin'* his *wittles*; sure*ly* he ain't a goin' to the *mowl country?* Less 'ope I ain't got the *cline*, mor; I *spooze* I shall het-a-git a bottle o' *stuff* from the doctor's, for I don't want to keep a *takin' on* a' this manner. Wot, *fussickin out* agin, Maria? Yow look as if yow a got a *takin' job.* You're right, I *thowt* I did heer the *door knock.* Well you a now ketched me *all up at Harwich,* so I doant like to *arst* ye in, *beside* I ain't got nothin' for tea only a little salary wot's *right clung*; why, *lawks*, the fire is nearly out for want of a *chife o'coal,* and I ain't had time yet to fill the coolshute. Is that yar little dawg keep a *yappin'?* No—that belong to owd "*Sondy*" acrost the way. I sometimes myself can't tell *which is which*, but yow jest lerrim off the string, mine is all *rip and tare* while the t'other is a *drawlatchin'* sort of a customer; hae? well, thankee we're all kinder *middlin'*, baaby annall; only my husband he felt like a *downpin* when he gorrup; *howsomever* he managed to eat a little *saample* for his brakfest and yow know he on't give up till he's fooss'd to 't; well there we fare to stan' here like *num' cnaance,* so we do.

FRED. R. FORSTER.

Can any of your contributors to this most interesting correspondence give the origin of the term main. "Lor bor, I coun't ate my maate so, I likes it *in the main.*" I was dining in a restaurant in Norwich recently and drew the waiter's attention to the fact that some beef he brought was nearly raw: to which he replied, "I'll change it if you wish—it is rather in the *main.*" A. J. G.

In the main means the same as *in the rear,* and is applied to underdone meat. We believe people ask for it *in the main* because *in the main* means "in the middle," where the meat is likely to be least cooked. Meat well cooked is said to be *home-done.*
—ED. *N.N.*

EAST ANGLIAN BIRDS.

I am anxious to collect the various local names by which our British birds are known, and therefore, with your kind permission, will take advantage of the present correspondence to give those which I have culled fron various sources. I have affixed authors' names to those words which I have not myself heard used, and shall be very glad to receive any additions to the list. So long as the word is now used in East Anglia to desciibe a certain bird it need not, for my purpose, be restricted to the county. In fact I doubt whether the following list contains a purely Norfolk word at all. Even "Pudden-poke" is used in Suffolk, and according to Johnson's Dictionary, poke means " a sack in the north of England, Camden; *pocca*, Sax. *poke*, Icel." Olf or ulph is also common in the sister county, and "Harnsei" is only a shortened form of Hernshaw. Arps, Scamels, and Mows I have not met with, nor can I find a derivation for. The term Reed Pheasant still survives in Essex (Miller Christy), and the Norfolk Plover is known as such elsewhere, and breeds as frequently perhaps in other counties as it does with us. It will be noticed that the names given to some birds are descriptive of their peculiar make or markings, note or nest, flight or food, habitat or time of arrival. Those people who talk of May Birds and Danish Crows are no believers in the lately revived theory of the hibernation of birds (*c.f.* "Migration of Birds," Charles Dixon, 1892), although some restrict the limits of the seasonal flight of the last mentioned, and dub him only Kentishman. It is remarkable how very few birds are distinctively known by our villagers except in the neighbourhood of a Grammar School ; birds' eggs there finding a ready sale. Some of the marshmen, professional punt-gunners, and "paulkers" are among the most practical of naturalists, being able to distinguish "fowl" at any rate, not only by their note by day, but their wing sound at night. Numerous causes have combined to render many avian provincialisms obsolete. The high price of corn some fifty years ago caused much waste land to be drained, enclosed, and broken up (distance only lends enchantment, &c., to those "good·" old times). [A plan was formed for turning Hickling Broad into corn fields.] Game preserving has cut both ways; acting deleteriously upon raptorials, but affording the sanctuary of the coverts to smaller birds generally. The scarcity, even as occasional visitants, of such birds as the Avocet, *e.g.*, which used to breed in Norfolk, has caused their "proper" names to be forgotten. The ten-shilling license has increased the number of shooters, and the spread of education and accompanying knowledge of natural history—popularised through the Press—has increased the number of collectors and taxidermists. The scientific title is duly given to every specimen, and its price has "riz accordin'."

The impossibility of distinguishing "a hawk from a harnser" (on the wing at any rate) will soon be a pardonable ornithological offence from the very dearth of individuals upon which to excercise our powers of observation.

Alexandra Plovers—Kentish Plover (E. T. Booth).
Arps—Tufted Ducks (D. Girdlestone, Southwell.)
Bird—A partridge, " Ha' you many bads te year?" English Birds and French Birds, meaning English and French Partridges.
Blue Hawk—Hen Harrier, male.
Billy Whit—The Barn Owl—The bird of wit or wisdom ; also *Willie Whit* and *Billy Wix*.
Butcher Bird—Red-backed Shrike—From its habit of killing and "spitting" small birds and insects.
Barley Bird—Nightingale (Forby), Siskin (Miller Christy) arriving about barley sowing time.
Black Cap—Black Cap, and more usually the Marsh Tit.
Bottle Tom—Longtailed Tit, Featherpoke.
Bramble Finch—Brambling.
Bloodolf—Bullfinch.
Blue Rock, Rock Dow—The Stock Dove, Rock Dove not occurring in Norfolk.
Baldie Coot—Coot.
Black Goose—Bernicle and Brent Goose, or Brant.
Bargoose and Bargander—Bar, Sheld, Patched, male and female Sheldrake.
Black Duck—Scoters.
Black and White Pokers—Both Immature Golden Eye and Tufted Duck.
Black Poker—Tufted Duck.
Bluegill—Scamp Duck, also Greybacks, *c.f.*, "Trans. of Norfolk and Norwich Naturalists Society," 2, 397.
Blue Darr—Black Tern (Dar-dart?)
Bittewren—Bittern.
Black Curlew—Glossy Ibis.
Banjobill—Spoonbill (A. Patterson).
Caddie—Jackdaw (Jack! Cade?!!) Caddow.
Chit-Perl—Chit, small, Lesser Tern ; Sea Swallows and Mackerel Birds.

Cobs—Any of the larger Gulls.
Come-back—Guinea fowl. Female only calls " Come back ! "
Cow Bird—Yellow Wagtail, from frequenting cows at marsh for the purpose of insects attracted thereby.
'Coy Ducks—A small and loquacious breed of domesticated Ducks used for decoying purposes.
Crow—Rooks generally, I have actually heard " whose rooks as those crows?" *c.f.*, " crow scaring.
Draw-water King Harry, or King Harry Draw-water—The former from its being taught in captivity to draw water for itself with a thimble and chain.
Develing or *Devil Bird*—The swift, from its blackness and uncanny *tout ensemble*. Its note is a weird cry, and only as night approaches does it fly low enough to be specially noticed. It inhabits, for roosting and nesting purposes, high and lofty places (frequently church towers), and never alights upon the ground.
Doddy Wren—The Wren—doddy, diminutive - all teeney, tiny things are familiarly addressed and respected in Norfolk parlance, *c.f.*, " little old," old being a term of endearment, pitman, the petman, &c.
Dickey Bird or *Sea Pie*—Oyster Catcher. Dickey *c.f.*, slang for shirt-front. The black and white on breast being conspicuous in its uniting.
Didlymot—Guillemot, Willock (E. F. G.).
Dobchick—Little Grebe or Dabchick.
Englishman—English Partridge.
Fulfer—The Missel Thrush, but indiscriminately applied to the Redwing and Fieldfare as well.
Felt—Fieldfare. Not common (felt, to flock).
Firetail—Redstart, synonymous.
Fuzhacker—(Haccan, Sax., *c.f.*, hacker, a stammerer)—Made to do duty for Stone and Whinchat.
French Linnet—Twite (A. Patterson).
Frenchman—French Partridge, also Red Leg.
Golden Eagle—This is the name given to the immature White-tailed Eagles that from time to time occur in East Anglia.
Game Hawk—The Peregrine.
Guler, Goolie, and *Goldfinch* - Yellowhammer.
Greenolf—Greenfinch, Green Linnet, Greenie.
Goat Sucker or *Night Hawk*—Nightjar. The former name is dependent upon a popular fallacy, and the second is derived from its hawk-like flight.
Golden—Golden Plover.

Grey Goose—Grey Lag, Bean and Pink-footed Goose.
Golden Eyes—Tufted Ducks, immature.
Grey Gulls, Grey Cobs—Immature Black-backed or Herring Gulls.
Hay Jack—Whitethroat, Nettlecreeper.
Horned Owl—Long-eared Owl ⎫ These are only known
Brown Owl—Tawny Owl ⎬ generally to game-
 ⎭ keepers.
Hedge Betty—Hedge Sparrow and Hedge Spike (*spidzo* to chirp). Its note is said to betoken rain.
Herring Spink—Golden Crested Wren, from its sometimes alighting upon boats engaged in herring fishing during the period of autumnal migration.
Hoodie—Grey Crow, also, Norway Crows, Danish Crows, Kentishmen, and Carrion Crows.
Harnser or *Frank Heron Crane*—Common Heron, Hernshaw.
"I ha seen the rooses blume,
I ha seen the wiolet blow,
I ha seen the harnser fly high,
But I ha seen northin loike yow."
(Love sick swain to his inamorata).
Hart Duck or *Grey Duck* - Gadwall (Stevenson, Southwell, Lubbock ; Grey Duck also female of Mallard.)
Half Fowl—1, Teal and Widgeon ; 2, Diving Ducks.
Holland Goose—Solan Goose or Gannet, evidently a corruption of the former.
Jacks—Jack Snipe.
Kitties—Any of the smaller Gulls.
Laughing Goose—White-fronted Goose.
Little Mealy Duck—Longtailed Duck, female (E. T. Dowell, Southwell).
Little Rattlewing—Morillon (Bewick), immature ; Golden Eye (Paget, Yarmouth, 1834).
Loon—Loen, Dutch, Great-Crested Grebe, also Greeve.
Mesh Herrier—Marsh Harrier and Montagu's ditto.
Mavish — Thrush. The "h" is pronounced, especially in plural.
Mudlark—Rock Pipit.
Maybird, Titterel—Whimbrel, Jack Curlew.
Molberries—Skuas (E. T. Booth).
Norway Thrush—Redwing, not common.
Nope—Bullfinch [Ray], W. Rye, Drayton.
Norfolk Plover—Thick-knee, Stone Curlew.

Ostril or *Orstril*—Clearly a corruption of "Osprey," sometimes called the Fish Hawk.
Oxeye—The Great Tit.
Oxbird or *Stint*—Dunlin, the smaller waders are not often excluded.
Puddenpoke, Ground Oven, Oven Tit, Ovenbuilder—Willow Wren and Chiffchaff from shape of nest. That these two birds and their nests should be confounded is excusable since externally they are so much alike.
Pickcheese—Blue Tit, sometimes "Beebird" and Tomtit.
Polly Wash Dish—Pied or "Penny" Wagtail.
Pywipe—Pewit, Green Plover.
Pigmies—Curlew Sandpiper.
Pintail Smee—Pintail Duck.
Poker, Sandy Head, or *Sandy Headed Pokers*—Pochard, male sometimes called Redhead drake; female ditto, "Dunbird."
Perl—Perl, purl (?) to turn over, *c.f.*, he came a purler. Common Tern.
Ringtail—Hen Harrier, female.
Reed Pheasant—Bearded Tit.
Reed Sparrow—Reed Bunting.
Red Linnet - Common Linnet.
Ring Dow—Wood Pigeon. "Drop down the deke, bor, hinder come a dow;" deke may be a wet ditch or a dry one, but dike is always a wet one. Deke may also mean the bank, that is the earth thrown out in making the dike.
Red Leg - Redshank; also the French Partridge.
Red Knots—Knots in summer plumage; grey ditto in autumn, or immature.
Runners—Land and Water Rails.
Rattlewing—Golden Eye, adult.
Rattle Wings—Golden Eye, from the noise it makes in flight.
Shepherd's Bird—Wheatear (A. Patterson).
Sedgebird—Sedge Warbler } Sometimes not distin-
Reedbird—Reed Warbler } guished *inter se.*
Snow Fleck—Snow Bunting, fleck-flake, from its mottled plumage, and coming at snowtime.
Scribbling Finch—Corn or Common Bunting and the Yellowhammer, from the pencilling of their eggs.
Spink—Chaffinch, phonetic (*winc,* ancient British) *spidzo,* to chirp.
Spurrer—Sparrow.
Snakebird, Cuckoo's Mate—Wryneck. Snakebird

from its hissing note when disturbed on its nest, and Cuckoo's Mate because it arrives about the same time a the Cuckoo.

Stone Runner—Ring Dotterel.
Summer Snipe—Common Sandpiper.
Summer Lamb—Common Snipe, from its "drumming" or lambing in summer.
Shorel Duck—Shoveller, Shovelbill-drake.
Summer Teal—Garganey.
Smee—Widgeon, Smeeth Duck?
Sea Phaysant—Pintail (Sir T. Browne, Southwell); Longtailed Duck (E. T. Dowell, Southwell).
Sirce or *Smew*—The Smew, Weasel Duck (C. A. Johns).
Sawbill—Merganser and Goosander, generally the latter, which is also called by its proper name, with emphasis on second syllable.
Sprat Loon—Red-throated Diver.
Scoulton Cobs or *Puit*—Black-headed Gull, Mow. *c.f.*, Mow Creek, Wells (Colonel Fielden).
Titlark or *Ground Lark*—Meadow Pipit.
Turkey Buzzard or *Buzzard Hawk* or "*Great Old*"—The Rough-legged, Common, and Honey Buzzard, not generally distinguished.
Turtle Dow—Turtle Dove.
Tufted Golden Eye—Tufted Ducks, mature.
Teuke—Curlew, Whimbrel, and Godwit—but usually the Redshank—on the coast.
Windhover—The Kestrel.
Widgeon—At Blakeney, the Golden Eye (E. T. Dowell).
Weasel Duck—Smew (*Mustela variegata*), Sir T. Browne.
White-Eyed Poker—Ferruginous Duck.
Woodcock Owl—Short-eared Owl—So-called because it arrives here about the same time as the Woodcock.

Words connected with above subject:—

Dutch Nightingale—Frog (Spur) W. Rye.
Egging—Bird's nesting, especially applied to taking eggs of game.
Fen Nightingale—Frog (Forby).
Fat-hen—Goose grass, *Chenopodium album*. The seed of this weed is a favourite food of game birds and wild fowl, &c.
Gobbler or *Stag*—Cock Turkey over a year old.

Gay bird—Any bright-coloured bird—the male of any species.
Hopping Toads—Frogs, E. T. Booth; perhaps Natterjack Toads? (M.C.H.B.)
Huddle-me-Close—Sidebone.
Little Bäds—Fried Mice, given to children for whooping cough, and so called to deceive them.
March Birds or *Marsh Birds*—Frogs.
Nest Gulp—The smallest and weakest of a brood of nestlings (Forby).
Skipjack—The clavicle, merry thought, or wishing bone.
Up—A bird is said to be " up," or have his " bloom up," when in full breeding plumage.

M. C. H. BIRD.

The thanks of all local naturalists are due to the Rev. M. C. H. Bird for putting into such a portable compass the " Broad Norfolk" nicknames of our Norfolk birds. As there are a few others which might be added, it may not be thought superfluous to mention them.

Cuckoo's mate—Wryneck, " 'cause he comes with the t'other."
Cute—Coot. "There've been a *body* of *cutes* on Breydon since the Broads ha' *friz*."
Davelin—Swift, pronounced as if an "r" had a right to come between the "a" and "v."
Dottrel—Ring Plover, and I have heard it described as *dodlin*.
French marish—Redwing. Indeed, many folks really believe he left that excitable Republic to spend the winter with us.
Gullchaser—Skua. "Tha's all he is."
Hornpie.—Lapwing. He carries a crest or horn; and is pied to boot.
Mussel duck—Black Scoter. "The *mussel* ducks allers *lay* off the North Beach in the dead of winter."
Sandlinnet and *Sandlark*—Sanderling.
Scotch goose.—Brent goose. "The old *Scotch geese* allers show up in hard frost, but 'aint they shy!"
Shoe-horn and *Cobbler's awl*—Avocet.
Shovel-bill and *Spoonbill-duck*—Shoveller. "Lor', aint they a treat, when nicely cooked!"

Snowman—Snow bunting. Birdcatcher: "I *copt* a *swag* of *snowmen* yesterday, and some *tidy* white 'uns among 'em."
Stints—Dunlin, "there's a *rare mess* of *stints* on Breydon sometimes"
Water-hen—Moorhen, often pronounced with an "i" instead of "e."
Wil-ducks—Guillemot and Razorbill. "Can't they *skive* under water when they want tu!"
A. PATTERSON.

Allow me to send you a list to supplement that which appeared in your issue of yesterday signed "M. C. H. Bird" of local names of shore birds of the North Norfolk coast, which he omits.
Blue dar—Black Tern (E. Norfolk.)
Clinker—Avocet.
Cambridge Godwit—Greenshanks.
Cream-coloured Mow—Imm. of Glaucous, or Iceland gull.
Dipcere—Tern.
Didapper—Grebe.
Grey Mallard—Gadwall.
Green Plover, Pywipe—Peewit.
Loon or *Lowan*—Red-throated diver.
Mud Plover—Grey plover.
Magloon—Great Northern Diver.
Mow—Gull (in general.)
Parrotbeak—Puffin.
Rattlewings—Adult Goldeneye.
Stint—Dunlin.
Seapie—Oystercatcher.
Spoonbeak—Shoveller duck.
Steelduck—for imm. merganser.
Stone Runner—Ringed plover.
Skeleton, Mud Snipe, Martin Snipe - Green sand-piper
Scammell, Pick—Godwits. "I'll fetch three young scammels from the rock." Caliban, in "The Tempest."
TanglePicker—Turnstone.
Willie—Guillemot.

I have spelt these words phonetically, knowing no other way. It is worth noting how most of these local names point to some peculiarity in the habits, plumage, or voice; but for *skeleton, scammell, stint,* and *mow* I can assign no reason. E. W. DOWELL.

It would be very interesting if some person with the necessary leisure would make as complete a list as possible of the local names used by our Norfolk gunners and beachmen, many of which, although very expressive and even poetical, are fast dying out; the names also applied to many of the land birds are equally interesting. I have from time to time noted such as I have met with, but I am sorry to say not with any degree of industry. One great difficulty is the uncertain way in which these men pronounce the names of birds, and if any attempt is made at getting a more distinct utterance the result is always confusion; it thus happens that the phonetic spelling varies considerably, and sometimes there is quite a family of similar names, all evidently of the same origin. Thus the Black Guillemot is known as the *tysle, taiste, toyst*, and *tysty*. Referring to Mr. Dowell's list, I notice the same thing. "Dipeese" I have always interpreted "dip-ears" a very appropriate name for the terns, which are also called "Shrimp pickers." "Magloon" (probably the prefix means "large") is applied to the Great Northern Diver, which is also known as the Herring Loon, to distinguish it from its smaller relative, the Red-throated Diver, or "Sprat Loon." Scammell and pick for Godwits certainly are rather puzzling. The term "Pick" may refer to its mode of feeding. Thus the Turnstone is known as the "Tangle Picker," but that Scammell has any connection with the mysterious Scamel which Caliban promised to procure from the *rocks* I much doubt. Godwits do not breed on rocks but in marshes, and if we can imagine a printer's error (a not unfrequent occurrence even now-a-days) by which the letter "c" was made to do duty for "e" we have "Seamels" or Sea-gulls, which would seem to clear up the whole matter. I have heard many very pretty and descriptive names derived from the habits or notes of birds; thus the Snipe is known as the "Air Goat," "Heather Bleater," and "Summer Lamb;" the Little Grebe, "Dive-an-dop;" the Night-jar, "Razor-grinder," "Scissor-grinder," and Churn Owl; the Quail, "Wet-my-lip" (from its note); the Mistletoe Thrush, "Storm-cock," from its habit of singing in rough weather; the Kestrel, "Windhover," "Windfanner," highly descriptive of its graceful hovering flight; the Green Woodpecker, "Rainbird;" the Sheld-duck, "Burrow Duck," from its nesting in rabbit burrows; the Pintail Duck, "Caloo," or "Coal-and-Candlelight," from a fancied interpretation of its singular cry; the Lapwing, "Flapjack," and many others.

I do not think the following occur in either of the lists you have published:—

Bottley Bump, Bottle Bump, Bitour—Bittern.
Coble Bird or *Cobble Bird* - Hawfinch (Sir T. Browne)
Clod Bird, Bunt Lark—Common Bunting.
Coney Chuck, White Rump—Wheatear.
Dunnock—Hedge Sparrow.
Hobby Bird—Wryneck (Sir T. Browne).
Mealy Bird—Longtailed Duck.
Meshn Bird—Fieldfare.
Mouse Hawk, Woodcock. Owl—Short-eared Owl.
Popeler—Shoveller (Le Strange Household Book).
Sedge Marine—Sedge Warbler (F. Norgate).
Sea Dove—Little Auk.
Shovelard—Spoonbill (Sir T. Browne).
Spowe—Whimbrel (Le Strange Household Book).
S'ag—Common Wren.
Stone Falcon—Merlin.
Summer Teal, Crick - Gargany Teal.
White Nun - Smew.

As specimens of broad Norfolk I remember years ago in a village near Lynn hearing a woman tell her daughter to "put the gotch 'er the winden." A virago in the same old town was peculiarly inventive in her threats to her children, and I have heard her exclaim, "Yow maw Haryet, come yow hare; I'll pull yar liver-pin out for yow." Poor Harriet! on such occasions I have not unfrequently *heard* the blows inflicted with the "short brush." "*Go on*" is frequently used as an expression of surprise. "Why, go on, bor!" or it may in some cases be interpreted, "leave off," much depends upon the inflection.

T. SOUTHWELL.

I do not remember noticing in the "Broad Norfolk" bird names any of the following:—

Com. Sandpiper—*Shrieker*, on account of its note.
Fieldfare—*French Fulfer*.
Goldfinch—*King Harry, Thistlefinch*, and according to differences in throat markings — *Peathroat* and *Chiveller*.
Grey Plover—*Full-eyed Plover*, from its large eyes.

Green Sandpiper—*Black* Sandpiper; looks so when flying.
Grey-leg Goose—*Home-leg Goose*
Missel-thrush—*English Fulfer*.
Partridge—*Short*, on account of its build.
Stonechat and Whinchat—*Furzechucks*.
Starling — *Chimney-pot-plover* (good reason for why!)
Scaup (male)—*Grey-back*; correctly so.
Scaup (female) — *White-nosed Day-fowl*, from its white-banded forehead. A. P.

In the list of Norfolk birds given by Mr. Bird, and supplemented by Mr. Southwell, no mention is made of "The Spotted Fly-catcher, called "Wall Bird," common in the neighbourhood of Norwich, and very noticeable both from its note and its peculiar method of darting out from a branch or rail to seize its prey; nor of the "Nuthatch," commonly called "Creeper" or "Free Creeper." Mr. Bird gives the Norfolk name for Whinchat as "Fuzhacker." I have not heard it so called, the name I am familiar with is "Furchuck," which I take to be a corruption of Furze Chick.

Can any of your readers tell me whence certain specimens of the common domestic duck obtained the crest or "top-knot" which adorns their heads? I have from time to time seen various individuals so distinguished, but have never seen or heard of any breed to which it is peculiar, unless it be the Wild Crested Duck. Here are one or two additional specimens of Broad Norfolk. *Sneck*, a door-latch; *Wank*, usually used in half contemptuous, half good humoured way as, "What, did you do that for, you wank, you." I am sorry no one can explain "Woosh," my own opinion is that it is a "missing link," a survival of the language once common to horses, bipeds, &c.   J. PITCHER.

May I be allowed to add a line on the much vexed question of the meaning of the word *do*, used in opposition to the former clause of a sentence? It is simply another form of the word "though," and answers to the German *doch*. "Is there a rake on the premises?" I asked of the daughter of the farm-bailiff in whose house we were lodging. "Do—Father has got the key," was the reply, evidently equivalent to "Father has got the key, though!" implying that it could not be had without his permission. And in all sentences, however apparently ungrammatical, this will apply.

Spoult means brittle. The nursemaids used to put vinegar into "tuffey" (tough enough, no doubt, without it) to make it *spoult*. Wood too old or dry is apt to be *spoult*, and unfit for working.

Clung is used for fruit or vegetables which have been kept so long as to be flaccid; a malady most incident to cucumbers and gooseberries.

Mother appears on pickles and jams as a sort of whiteness on the top when fermentation has set in—called also a *hough*, and applicable to the appearance in certain cutaneous diseases.

Roke, *reek*, and *wrack* are all forms of the same word, indicating steam or cloud; Shakespeare alludes to cloud-capped palaces, dissolving into thin air, and "leaving not a wrack behind."

Your correspondents do not seem to be aware that the Yorkshire and Lancashire divisions of the fields are made of dry stones and called *dykes*. *Whin dykes*, too, are heard of. I knew a small lane, or *loke*, leading from a farmyard inclosed on both sides with a stone wall, and called "the dickey." This was near Banbury.

Don't ought is a favourite expression; but our people do not generally add "to." *Don't ought to* is used in many counties, and it is good Anglo-Saxon nevertheless.

The reply of a friend's coachman who was remonstrated with for certain irregularities may be amusing. "Well, ma'am! the truth is, I am like St. Paul. What I ought to do I don't do, and what I do do I don't ought."

A Yorkshire friend coming to reside in Norfolk was attracted by the sound of a continued tapping in his garden, and, inquiring the cause, was told, "It is northin, only the mavishes *napping* (or *knapping*) the dodmans." "But what are mavishes and what are dodmans?" was his reply. He recognised "knapping" from "knappeth the spear" in the Psalms.

I have not observed *malahacked* and *jammuck* amongst your correspondents' lists. I heard of a donkey purchased for little money on account of some injury; but it was not so malahacked as to be jammucked for all that."

Has any one heard now-a-days of a popular remedy for whooping cough, namely, pills made from the hair cut off the dark brown mark on the donkey's back, and called *Balaam's smite*, made up with butter or dripping, I believe? Also fried mice, always pronounced *meece*, or dragging a child through the space formed by a bramble grown at both ends. Four moles' feet, tied up in a bag, and worn round the neck are good for rheumatism, but it must be the forefeet which are to be worn in case of rheumatism in the arms, and hindfeet for the legs.—Hoping I have not been too garrulous, A NORFOLK WOMAN.

I notice that "A. G. D." in his letter to-day refers to an *olland* being frequently called a *layer* or *lay*. This is not quite correct. A *layer* or *lay* is the term applied to grass growing for hay from the time the barley is cut till it is well grown and almost ready to cut; and the term *olland* is applied to the land after the second crop of hay has been taken off. Amongst the words I have not yet seen in your paper are the following:— *Sanniken*, silly, foolish; *jumble*, porter and beer mixed; *danks*, tea leaves. A man once explained to me of two main drains in a heavy land field that *t'one come sarshen, t'other one go yin*. I have heard a wedding favour, *i.e.*, rosette, called a *gay* as well as flowers and pictures. I have also by me many letters from working men, which, as lessons in phonetic spelling, are as good as one can wish for, and I once received a letter on the envelope of which was written,
OCTIONARY.

Having been much interested in reading your correspondence on "Broad Norfolk," permit me to contribute my quota, and to observe that our Norfolk peasantry have been the conservators of many words that have been handed down since East Anglia was peopled by Saxons, Danes, and Norman invaders. *E.g.*, the other day I asked a person who was long in arrears to me when it would be convenient

to pay, at which he rather tartly told me I was not
"*Jarneck.*" Some friend will perhaps interpret.
Another, a tenant in trade, told me that business
was so down that he should "*Jack up.*"
A Norfolk man may generally be spotted by his
brogue; for instance, I was once at an inn-room in a
small town in Scotland, where sat a solitary
gentleman eating his dinner. He suddenly arose
and rang the bell. Waiter put in his appearance,
a dirty napkin on his arm. "Waiter, have you got
any *taters?*" I interrupted. "Bor, yew are Norfolk."
And the stranger replied, "So are yew, bor." After
further confab he informed me that he "did in the
beut and shue line, and hailed from Norwich."
Rustic ignorance, too, is conspicuous. I was walking
near Sandringham on a sketching excursion, and
trying to depict some ruins. A boy tending some pigs
was near me. On asking the youth in what parish
the ruins were he, pitying my ignorance, informed me,
"Don't yer see they beant in no parish; they be in a
feld."
I know Forby's "Vocabulary of East Anglia" is an
authority, but something in the shape of an addenda
would be of value to preserve these quaint old words.
W. C. S.

The curious expressions appearing in the *Press*
under the heading of "Broad Norfolk" have been
numerous, yet some have escaped the notice of previous
writers. Some people may look upon this correspondence as a lot of *squit and slaver* (nonsense), but
they need not look "*as sour as wadges*" about it.
Having *gun* (given) us the opportunity of " airing our
lingo," which we *haa'nt* (have not) had lately, " *I'le
git treu* (I will get through) mine in a *jiffey* (a short
space of time). There seems to be such a *cholder*
(quantity) of these phrases, but I think we true Norfolk *jhaps* (fellows) will *gie yow all onem* in time:
When I went to school the boys brought
their *skran* (dinner) with them. Some would
have *schwad* (pork cheese or brawn). But I won't go
on in this fashion. *Flopped* is a word in common use,
meaning thrown down. *Crinkley crankley like* is
explained by the compound word " zig-zag."
Children *jiffle* or *jidgett* about, and you might as well

"*gape aginst a red hot oven as to stop em.*" If insinuating, I have been asked "*what are yer minten at*"—this may mean *hinting*. In buying herrings I have heard Norfolk people ask for either "*miltz*" or *dotts*, the latter probably owing to the formation of the roe, which appears to be made up of specks or dots. I find, however, that the use of *u* for *o* and *oo* as in *butes, spune*, &c., is more marked in *Norwich* than outside of it.

T. P. S.

Verily we shall soon have a recorded language peculiarly our own. In order, as we say, to keep the pot a bilin, I send a further list of words in daily use (in East Norfolk).

Slew, slewed, this word does not (with us) mean a departure from temperance principles, it is used thus: "Let's *slew* the elevator round."

Ferry fake, impudent prying. What are you ferry faken arter?

Gulcher, to fall heavily. "It came down a *gulcher*."

Morfrey, an hermaphrodite—agricultural carriage, such as tumblers for instance.

Buttress, an implement used by blacksmiths for paring hoofs of horses.

Meetiners, Protestant Dissenters.

Go tu meetin clothes, the Sunday or best suit.

Titty totty, extremely tiny.

Titty-ma-torter, a see-saw, or a see-saw action.

Sunk, ill cooked food. "Here's a sunk to sit down to."

An old man once addressed his master, a shopkeeper, who was busily engaged in putting the price to some goods, with the following request—"*Mar kum tru?*" "I am," said the employer. "Yes, sur," said Jemmy, "but mar kum tru, sir?" After a little "argerfying" it turned out that the inquiry really was "May I come through?"—that is, pass by the counter, and not "Mark them true." At prayer meetings I have sometimes heard expressions that would puzzle theologians. One good old man always asked that he might be "blowed up like a grain o' mustard seed," which we somehow imagined was a desire that his spiritual graces might bloom (blow) with the celerity of the seed mentioned. It was only the other day I heard an irate rustic, with infinite scorn, express it as his opinion that if he "warn't much of a *rithmetickerer* he knowed wot tu and tu wos." Possibly he had heard much of arithmetic from his grandchildren attending the Board "schule." W.H.C.

If you are not surfeited with "Broad Norfolk" I offer the following. Many of the so-called "Broad Norfolk" words which have been referred to in your correspondence are proper words, and in general use throughout a great part of the Kingdom, but somewhat corrupted in pronunciation.

Anser, Harnser, for *Heron* (*pron. Hern*). The former is the scientific name of the tribe of which the Heron is a member. Anser fat is said to be an infallible cure for incurable diseases, probably from the fact that the Heron is nothing but skin and bone. In this respect it is akin to pigeon's milk, so much in request on the 1st of April.

Mavis, a thrush, called a grey bird in Devonshire, where the blackbird is sometimes called a black thrush.

Cosset, Coeset, a lamb, &c., brought up by hand—*Spenser.* [Bailey.]

Cub-baw. A young Frenchman many years ago came to England, and applied himself to the study of the language and idioms. He heard a Norfolk farmer shout "Cub-baw!" to his lad, who was slow in bringing his horse. The pocket dictionary was brought into requisition without effect. "What did he say?" says the Frenchman to a friend; "I've looked through C and K and can't find anything like it." This was the first occasion that M. du Maurier (for he it was) heard the Norfolk pronunciation of "Come boy."

Caddow, a Jackdaw, or chough, *Norf.* [Bailey], sometimes called "*Cadder.*" I suppose you have heard the tale of Bishop Stanley and "Jim Crow's cadders."

Cupbear, should be "*Come hither,*" or "*Come hither wi' ye.*" When a teamman leads his horse he is on the left, or near side; therefore the expression would mean "turn to the left." *Whish,* or *whosh,* a frightening sound, to drive the horse to the right. "*Come hither wi' ye*" is used in the west of England, but I have never heard "*whish*" out of Norfolk.

Contain is sometimes used for "detain," *e.g.*, "I won't contain you."

Dang, darn.—The first word seems to be Norfolk,

the other is heard in other places. Both words may be as near an approach to a great big D as politeness would permit.

Dow, dove. This is in use in the north of England and in Scotland.

Deficiency, for sufficiency. Heard at a village tea meeting. "Do 'ee have another cup of tea, Mr. Lemon." [He had already had 18.] "No thank'ee marm, I've had quite a deficiency."

Enow, plural of *enough* ["Walker's Dictionary."] Used elsewhere.

Fysty, foisty. Spoken of food when going bad or mouldy. *Fust*, a strong smell, as that of a mouldy barrel. *Fustiness*, mouldiness, stink. *Fusty*, smelling mouldy. [Walker.]

Keeler, a shallow tub—query from "Cooler."

Hulver, for holly (hulfere, holly, "Chaucer")—Query, wholly green, always green, wholly-vert. A shrub that is green in winter and summer.

Half-rock, half-wit....

Hutkin, hudkin, query hoodkin, dim. of hood; a covering for a cut finger.

Gaffer, good father, *Saxon*, used all over the kingdom.

Mentle, Mantle, a working apron.

Mawkin, a figure set up to scare birds. *Malkin* (of *Mall*, contrac. of *Mary*, and *kin*, or *mannikin*), a sort of mop or shovel for sweeping an oven. [Bailey]. "*Malkintrash*," one in a rueful dress, enough to fright one [Bailey]. "*Crimalkin*," lit. a *grey malkin*; an old cat [*gray*, and *malkin*, a dirty drab, a corruption of *Moll* or *Mary*. "Chambers's Dictionary."] *Dudman*, a malkin, or scarecrow, a hobgoblin, a spright [Bailey].

Plantain, plantation.

Pightle, alias *Picle, Pictellum*, a small parcel of land inclosed with a hedge, which the common people of England do, in some places, call a *Pingle*, and may perhaps be derived from the Italian word Picciola, *i. parvus* ["Dr. Cowel's Dictionary, 1708].

Pawk, poke (?)

Pakenose, an inquisitive person, pokenose (?)

Pulk hole. Pulla, a pool or lake of standing water, whence a *pulk* is a small pond or hole of standing water. ["Blomefield's Norfolk," vol. III., p. 271. Title, "Pulham."]

Romant, a corruption of romance, a suggestion that

the person who has "romanted" has drawn on his imagination.

Sharm, Shawm (?). From its sound it would seem to infer a noisy instrument; but I believe the shawm was a stringed instrument.

Swaling, a candle wasting from draught. "The candle was swaling in the wind."

Skute, a part of a field in the shape of a shield (?), from *scutum* (Latin), a shield.

A Sisserara, does this refer to a blow such as Jael dealt Sisera?

Sag, to hang down on one side. [Bailey.]

Sidus, sideways.

Thew and *snew*. An old shepherd once said to me, "First it *blew*, then it *snew*, then it *thew*, and then it turned round and *friz*." E. B. POMEROY.

Among the words not already mentioned may be included *shail*, which, as well as *cail*, means to throw, more especially, I think, a missile at any living creature; and *jannick*, fair or candid, as, for instance, "I hope he will be jannick, and tell the whole truth about the matter." Is *jannick* a corruption of *genuine?*— RAMBLER.

Though rather late in the day, I venture to send you a small contribution on this subject. When a boy I constantly heard a curious expression which I find it somewhat difficult to describe. It was a prefix like the word "saint," only pronounced short, thus, "Don't *s'nt* antickin like that, don't." The word "mischievous" is commonly pronounced *mischeevous*, with the accent on the second syllable, and I have heard it used in the sense of active and restless, as "I'm a *mischeevous* sort of man, and must be doing something." The word *terrify* is, I believe, often used in the sense of tease, as "The flies *terrify* the hoss." I was pleased to see the word *sluss* in one of your correspondent's letters, as it seems to me to be the true Norfolk pronunciation; but the word *mavis*, mentioned earlier, I have always heard called *mavish*, and *come-arther* and *whoosh* seem to my recollection the sounds of the guiding words of the driver of a waggon to his horses. I once heard the gable end of a house called the *gavel* end, and this struck me, as there is a mountain in Cumberland commonly called Great Gable, but described in a guide book as Great *Gavel*, the explanation of the name being that it is like the gable end of a house. What is now called Boxing Day was in my young time called *Offering* Day, and as their Christmas boxes are said to have originally been religious gifts, there may be a trace of this origin in the name of the day. There is one other point I should like to mention. I have often noticed that strangers to this county have a tendency to pronounce names of places ending with "*ham*" as if they ended with "*sham*." Thus they call Aylsham *Ayl-sham*, instead of Aylsham, as it should be, and as I believe it would be called by natives of the place, unless they have been "educated" out of it. This is of some importance, because the new pronunciation destroys the historical value of the name. E.

The following expressions struck me as being peculiar to Norfolk when I first came to reside in the county. For instance, when the church bell is tolling for the dead, I have been asked, "Who the bell is *out* for?" Do you know so and so? "I know him *to see to.*" For next morning you often hear "*next day morn.*" J. C. S.

I don't remember having seen the following odd words in your interesting correspondence. I have heard them used in different parts of this county all my life. A man went fishing and caught a *corker* and a *whopper*, meaning a large fish; another shot an *old sea mow*. A gardener told me one day, "I see our old missus this mornin', and she was right *yipper*, meaning in good spirits. Other phrases are to go *fribbling* and *finnickin* or *grubbing* about for *now't*, to be *trapen* about when it *smurs* of rain, and then go home and have a *few* gruel or broth to keep the cold out; to have a hot *dannock* for tea (a piece of dough baked in the frying pan as you would a pancake). There appears to be no end of these odd expressions, but a country village amongst the old folk is the place to hear them.

LAWK-A-DAISY-ME.

BROAD NORFOLK.

On consulting my note book, in which I jot down such little matters of personal observation, I find a few phrases which may not yet have appeared in this correspondence. Several of the so-called words that have been given are combinations, and could never rightly appear in any vocabulary.

I observe a few common words with an unusual application, such are *know* used as a noun, as "to lose one's know;" *rise*, in the sense of "raise;" *might*, as a noun, as in "a might of corn;" *welt*, to droop; *fence* for hedge; *gain* and *ungain*, convenient, &c.; *lash*, cold, raw; *clutch*, a seat of eggs; and *flat*, as in "flat milk." The word *jumble* may be merely slang. A little girl came running up to me one day, and with intonation and accent that can never be expressed on paper, said, "Oh! I have had such a ride in Mr. Blackburn's dickey caat, that went so fast, that it jumble right up agen the deke."

Also a few peculiar words; such are *ringe*, meaning a row or ridge; *scocker*, a verb expressing the breaking or bursting of the bark of a tree; *snew*, a noose; *shacking*, turning out pigs to gather stray ears in a harvest field.

One might notice also such expressions as *perk* for perch, and *wanten* for wanted. "Fosse," mentioned by one of your correspondents, is familiar in Lincolnshire.
R. G. W. TUCKER.

I don't know if my explanation will be satisfactory to your correspondent "M. C. H. Bird," as I am prepared with no proof. I may say, however, that when a lad my father informed me that in his young days the three Miss Pograms were prominent characters in a novel much read at the time. They were Nonconformists of a very sanctimonious type; hence, in ridicule, it is to be feared, Dissenters came to be spoken of as *Pograms*, and their chapel as a *Pograms-shop.*

Amongst the instances of Norfolk expressions I have not noticed in your coloumns *hawky*, a harvest frolic. If I mistake not I have met with this term in Bloomfield's "Farmer's Boy." W. N.

Your various correspondents are getting together quite a copious vocabulary of the words and phrases peculiar to our own and our sister county, Suffolk. So far, however, I have not noticed any allusion to two words in very general use—one descriptive of a fretful baby, who is said to be "*sannicking*," and the other of a handy man in amateur carpentering, &c., who is complimentarily referred to as a good "*jimpsener*." I spell both words phonetically, not being acquainted with any other mode.

More than one of the letters published under this heading give *mavis* as a Norfolk word. This is certainly good Lowland Scottish as well as Norfolk. Witness the adorer of "Bonnie Mary of Argyle," who used to hear

> The *mavis* singing
> It's love-song to the morn.

Scott also commences one of his minor lays with—

> 'Tis merry, 'tis merry, in good greenwood,
> When *mavis* and merle are singing—

and many other references to the thrush under the name of "mavis" might be quoted.

The distinguishing characteristics of East Anglian patois, however, are the suppression of the letter "r" when it comes after a vowel, and, less frequently, of the "g" final. For instance, in the "*Cawn*" Hall on any Saturday one is not unlikely to be made the recipient of a communication somewhat in this strain :— "Sam '*Panter's*' co' bolted this '*maunin*,' and broke the '*hahness*' and smashed the '*caht*.'"

PHARAOH.—

If your space will admit I shall be glad if you will insert the following instances of "Broad" language which I have not already seen mentioned in the correspondence on the subject :—

Bishimer or *fishimer*, the ant.
Unsensed, rendered insensible.
Kicking up a row, talking loudly to the annoyance of others.
Springy, a little the worse for drink.
Fleet, of little depth, as "a *fleet* dish."
Heel, remains of tobacco left in a pipe after smoking.
Click, to throw—as "I'll *click* a stone into the dog."
I *gathered* myself up, I rose up (after being thrown down on the ground from any cause).

Grained. The author of "Giles's Trip to London" calls this "*greened,*" but "*grained*" I have always heard in this district.

My cold is *breaking a bit* refers to convalescence after a cold. I heard an old lady ask for a "*deceit*" the other day, meaning " a receipt."

Some pronunciations of scientific terms are peculiar. Carbonate of soda becomes *Carpenter's soda*, and Iodine, *Arradeen*. "ALPHA."

Has anyone noticed the Norfolk peculiarity of using more verbs than in any other counties, especially as regards *do, did,* and *have?* Thus " he didn't ought to do it ; " " he didn't ought to have done it," &c. ? Many persons supposed to be educated make this mistake as well as uneducated people, who probably would say " *du,* he didn't ought to have done it." A. D.

I have not seen in your very interesting correspondence reference yet to the word *stove,* meaning to fumigate. As for the word *dullah,* I once heard it used in the following expression :—" If you don't leave off that ther dullah I'll cop you into the deke's holl and leave you there to blar !" There were the words of a sister to her little brother. Have you had the word *lether,* meaning ladder ! I heard it once used in this way—" Hain the lether." T. T.

I have been very much interested in the correspondence on this subject in the *Daily Press.* I am a Norfolk man, and have lived in West, South, and North Norfolk, and have noticed varieties of dialect peculiar to each division of the county. On my return to the county, after many years' absence, I listen with renewed delight to the old expressions, many of which I had almost forgotten. Thirty years ago I could have given you a formidable list of them. I have not noticed that any of your correspondents have mentioned the use of the word *happened* as signifying " met." " I *happened* with him *at mine*," or " I met him at my house." Here we have the French " chêznous." " He often come *to mine, ollus* of a Sunday."

I heard a keeper say many years ago of a wounded partridge, "There-a-go, *cherubidin'* along."

Norfolk people are fond of using long words of which they do not know the meaning, as one of your correspondents illustrated by the use of the word "*corroborate*" instead of "*correspond*."

The Norfolk oath takes various forms, always senseless, but probably derived from the same origin. A keeper had put a ferret into a rabbit's hole, and after listening at the mouth of the hole for some minutes, jumped up ejaculating as he brushed his ear, "*Kinsarm* them there *pishmires!*" or "Confound those "*Ants!*" which had got into his ear. "You don't *want* to do so-and-so," or "you've *no call* to do this or that," for "you need not," &c. "*Put on parts*" for "give himself airs." "Don't *act*," for "don't play tricks."

The *vowel* is nearly always put in the wrong place, or altered. "Woilet" for "violet," "sakele" for "seakale," "lebarneum" for "laburnum." "laloch" for "lilac," "christmas anthems" for "chrysanthemums," and "midsummer anthems" for "*mesambrianthemums.*" *V* is always changed to *W*. A woman speaking of her husband, who was an invalid, said, "He've no appetite to speak *on* (for *of*), but he can eat anything that *cum of a nonplush*-like" or "unexpectedly." A Norfolk person is never *well,* but "middlin," or "nicely," or "good tidily." Titles are *incomprehensible*, and can never by any means be made intelligible to a Norfolk labourer, or even the more or less educated middle class. A peer of the realm, or a baronet, or a knight makes no difference ; they *cannot* understand, and always speak of them as *Mr.*— "*Mr.* Lord So-and-so." A squire's wife they will often dub as "*Lady* So-and-so," because they consider she ought to have a higher title than themselves.

The teamman often says "Cum-hare—whooesht—holt" (or stop) all in one breath, as the horse moves a little too much to the right or left. Vowels I have said are altered. "Herbert" is pronounced "*Harbert.*" It is impossible to write the pronunciation of "now" or "dow" (for dove) phonetically ; you cannot express the contraction or mincing of the vowel. "Tree threes" for "Three trees" is quite unaccountable.

No other peculiarities occur to me at this moment, but if you will allow me, I will write again. Lady

Augusta Noel (daughter of the late Lord Albemarle) has some beautiful genuine Norfolk stories in her various charming books, not only correct in expression, but *idiom*; indeed, I recognise many old friends in her stories, picked up no doubt when visiting the poor in the neighbourhood of Quidenham. RECTOR.

We het to trosh a wate stack to-morrow, so our master sa he ha seen the chaps abou rit. So help ma tater, yinder she come some stroke down our loke. Thirs the byler, drum, and funky (a term for the three parts, engine, barnworks, and elevator). You must get the chaps to come that are hulling the slus and mud out of the holl agin the mash deek, as we must trosh in the morning. As sune as we start the straw must be hulled and chucked about the yards, cause they are in a woful state, and you be sure dont lave the gate undun, as them old hogs will hike out and sune stale into the garden and 'stry no end of roisbery canes and bushes and rute up the taters like hunting. That I know ont sute the old chap (master), whose temper is as short as picrust, and will sune nab the rust when things go ungain. A. B. C.

Some years ago when I was acting as Under-Sheriff of the County we had in the witness-box a marshman whose dialect so puzzled Lord Chief Justice Cockburn, that he requested me to stand by his side and translate the evidence in order that he might get his notes correct. Going home with his lordship in the carriage, I ventured to suggest that the witness referred to seemed to be quite unintelligible, and asked his lordship what he thought of the Suffolk dialect. His very characteristic reply was I always call Suffolk " Norfolk set to music." AN EX-UNDER-SHERIFF.

One of your correspondents the other day said he had heard a thorough-going Norfolk man talk about a certain drain, which he said *came sarshen*, meaning, I suppose, its course took a slanting direction. I have heard what no doubt in reality is the

D

same word, pronounced *sosh*, used, for example, when a field of corn (probably because of its being laid) has to be mown from one corner across to the other, instead of in a direction parallel to the hedge rows. "Soshen," I dare say, is "broader" than "sarshen." I have heard an order given to "throw the old deke down and use the *thorn-bulls* for firing," "bulls" denoting live or dead stubs. A very curious word which you might hear in the South Walsham neighbourhood is *skinker*, the equivalent for which seems to be "a distributer." Thus, supposing anybody brought a can of beer into a harvest field and poured the ale out for the men, some "dry" labourer would very likely chaff him with the remark, "Come, bor, you are a slow skinker." After the usual share has gone round any beer that remains is called "skinker's 'lowance." *Crick* is another word, meaning water-dike. A day or two ago a rustic was describing to me the habits of the gulls or sea-kitties. He used the phrase "swaling and twizzling about" to express the strange pitching and tossing of these birds—terms which at the time I thought far more vivid than words we should naturally have employed. An odd phrase oft used in Norfolk is *That's all me eye and Betty Martin*, denoting the speaker's decided dissent from any desire or opinion expressed. B. B.

At the risk of troubling you I beg to forward a few more specimens in daily use in East Norfolk. I do hope the outcome of this most interesting correspondence will be that you will publish our language in its entirety in book form, so that it may be preserved :—*Hingles* for hinges, "The door is blowed off the hingles." If your correspondent "West Norfolk" wishes to hear the East Norfolk *u* for *oo* in all its purity let him listen to an old parish clerk our way give out the following hymn :—

As pants the hart for culin streams.

Another word is used by this official which is most common amongst us, *faut*—fault. In the Confession Billy gives us the pure *native*, "Speer thou them which cornfess theer fauts," and also "ere" for "are," "Restore thou them that ere penitent." Amongst trades we have *kiddier*, a pork butcher; *knacker*, a harness maker. In London, as I am aware, a knacker is a horse slaughterer. Is not a *Tom* and *Jerry Shop* a general shop with a beer license ?   W. H. C.

As a native I have been much interested in the correspondence on the above subject; but after all I think a stranger could form no idea of the beauty (!) of our dialect unless he could hear and see a native of each district talk it. There are words used in one locality quite different from another. As to the word *deke*, I can quite understand a man gittin' up a' th' deke to luk over the hedge inter th' holl a' th' tother side. I fancy some of the correspondents are not very well up in their subject, as one says, "a conversation is often carried on across a ten acre field." I wonder if he knows how far that would be. I should say across a two acre pightle would be a fair distance to carry on any sort of conversation. Another says, "Have you dug any early potatoes t'year?" In broad Norfolk it would be " Ha yow tuk up na' airly taters t'year ? "   " No, mi ould wumman grubb'd sum owt a' wun rute, an' thay're hardly fit." I have heard Aylsham called *Els-ham*, *El-sham*, and *Ailsham*, and Foulsham *Foul-sham*. In many cases the yokel knows what the words are in dictionary English, although he speaks them in broad Norfolk. I have been in different parts of England, and in many places I have heard the Queen's English murdered more than it is in good old
EAST NORFOLK.

The expression "dare say" is pronounced *da' say*, and, curiously enough, is made to signify the exact reverse of its usual meaning, for most persons when they hear some intelligence which they quite expected to hear, exclaim, " Ah ! I dare say ; " while, on the other hand, if you impart some very surprising news to a Norfolk villager, he will most likely hold up his hands in amazement and cry, " Why ! da' say! " I believe this is also common to Suffolk.   R. L.

May I venture to point out a few localisms which I think have not been noticed in the

"Broad Norfolk" correspondence. "Solid, bor, solid!" meaning in one's usual health; "That would puzzle Acabo;" "If I *ha'nt* a kilt har;" "If-so-bein' yow carnt go;" "I'll sune rightside ye"—(to a disobedient child); "The grass is *lash*"—applied to young pasturage in spring; *telled* for told; "Look-a-haar;" "I 'ont het!" (I won't have it); "D' yow dut" (do it). *Duse-a-bit* is not from "How-so be it," as one of your correspondents thinks, and as a line in the following will show :—

NUSS AT THE HALL.

Like to git merried? Well, yessir, I a-bin a-thinkin' about it,
That is, if Sairey 'll ha' me, but sometimes I kinder doubt it.
Wot's that you're a-takin' yar pen out for? Yow're arter writin' a taale!
Will I drink yar health? Well, thank ye, I doant mind a a glaarse o' aale.
You haint sin Sairey? Well, bor, I'd like you to see har, tha's all;
She's a laady bred, though on'y a nuss, up yinder there, at the ball;
And when we are out o' Sundays—you shud see my Sairy an' I,
Why, I fare like a fule beside har, she carry harself so high!
Can I put my trust in Sairey? Well, you see, 'tis like this haar:—
There's a coachman chap at our paarson's, he abin there only to-year,
And he's kinder sweet upon Sairey; but lor, sir, that aint no use;
For she like a chap that can talk—an' he carn't say bo tu a guse!
But there's suffin about his looks. I don't see what it can be;
And Sairey du garp at him sometimes, though she know that doant suit me.
Well, I met the sawney, and nabb'd him by the collar o' his coat;
An', ses I, "Yew ort to be quaggled with a halter round yar troat;
The duse-a-bit, yow are winkin' an' maakin' mouths at Sal,
Yow 'n I'll fall out i' ye du, bor, for I'm goin' to merry that gal;
And a fule wi a buzzle-hid like yars—now, doant yow dar me tut,
My munkey is up, I tell ye, an' yow'll girra lift with my fut.
For yar *hid* is tu hard for punchin';" but he kinder larfed, and sed,
"Go on, you're a jokin', Johnny—yow dussent punch my hed"
Lor, I up and catch'd him a rum'un! I reckon his hid wuz sore,

Least-ways, he haint bin comin' his tricks wi' Sairey no
  more,
And I think, if ever she fancied him, when Sairey cum
  to see
How I luther'd his hide, she'll repent on't, and git harself
  spliced to me.
For Sally is none o' yar dollops, she aint no dawdlin' slut,
With har faace all a-muck an' untidy—like a sow an' nine
  pigs in a rut;
She's a slap-up mawther, I te'l ye, and—lawk-a-daisy me!
I well might be torken about her, for, dang it—why, *haar
  she be*!
                                                    E. HEWETT

The articles and letters in your recent issues on "Broad Norfolk" are most interesting, and I should like to say a word on the point raised by "Joskin" in last Tuesday's paper, where he says that we do not often hear of a Norfolk man being recognised by his brogue. This arises, I am inclined to think, more from the circumstance that such events are not recorded rather than that they do not occur.

I am myself a native of the "City of Gardens," but left it thirty-eight years ago, and have only been there once since, viz., at "Festival" time, 1863. During the interval I have, in consequence of my connection with one of the departments of our Army, lived at many different places, both at home and abroad, and I think I am right in saying that in every one of them I have been recognised as a Norfolk man simply from my speech. The last instance may suffice, which was that shortly after my joining my present station, I was introduced to the Town Clerk. Almost as soon as I spoke he said, "Pardon me, but from what part of Norfolk do you come?" he himself, I found, having been born in Surrey Street, Norwich. Now, as I may, without vanity, lay claim to be considered a well-educated man, and thus not given to "provincialisms," and as my experience is somewhat cosmopolitan, I think that the incident above mentioned may be worth recording (and I doubt not there might be hundreds, or thousands, of similar ones), as showing how one's early associations with the East Anglian capital still cling around us, although two-thirds of our life have been spent away from the old city; indeed, the problem is as interesting as those your chess editor gives us week by week, only that I am unable to solve it so easily as I can the latter.
                                            W. SHAW LEEST.

know that before the School Board came into operation children at the age of seven or eight years were sent into the fields to scare birds or to gather stones at so much per bushel, without ever having had the opportunity of learning the alphabet, that they should call a potato a "*tater*" and tobacco "*bacca*," &c. I am glad to think that many of your correspondents have had the advantage of a grammar or School Board education, and know how to avoid the errors which the poor and uneducated Norfolk and Suffolk labourers have fallen into. L. J.

"Car woo! Car woo! Here come the clappers to knock ye down backards and halle car woo." About fifty-five years ago I resided at Thetford. It was the custom round about there to have boys in the corn fields to frighten away the birds. They did so by shouting out the above words, and at the same time using the clappers, which consisted of thin pieces of wood fastened to a handle, which when shaken caused a loud rattling noise. The boys were called "crow keepers."

Should you consider the above quoted example sufficiently broad Norfolk, kindly insert it.
JNO. HOLLAND.

The following eccentricities will probably interest your East Anglian readers :—*Roaches*—signifies sweets (this word is far more popular than *cooshies*); *arms and legs*—home-brewed beer (this term implies that this beer has no body in it); *ear*—handle; *kit*—milk can; *lug*—ear; *hild*—yeast; *jangle*—to argue; *hulk*—to clean a rabbit or hare. I join with many other readers in hoping that you will produce a pamphlet on the above subject.
HERBERT ANDREWS.

The articles and correspondence in your columns on this subject have been most interesting to me and many friends, and I hope when they are concluded you will publish them in a reprint.

Another kindred subject is comprised in the names of fields, roads, &c., containing veritable "mines" of historical and traditional information. The names of fields were well treated of in a recent number of the Norfolk and Norwich Archæological Society's publications, but by no means exhaustively, and I hope you may see your way to make your columns the means of rescuing from oblivion the wealth of history and tradition represented in these names.

EDWARD T. AYERS.

While fishing close to Barton Broad with a friend, I happened to let my line drag along the bottom, when to my surprise a countryman near gave me the advice " You shud fleeten yar fut line, bor." This I presume meant not to fish quite so deep.

E. KENDALL.

" Het Varke " asked the other day for the meaning of *corder*, but gave no context, or example of the way in which the word was used. I have never heard it myself, nor can I find it " registered " anywhere. We have a *cord* of faggots, but this does not appear to be a purely East Anglian expression, for Evelyn used it in Surrey for " a quantity of wood supposed to be measured with a cord (*chorda*, Latin). It is just possible that "corder" may have been written in mistake for " golder "—loud laughter, or Gord a'mercy—or Gord a'mighty—or " colder "—rubbish. A friend suggested *si vis* or *si velis* as the derivation of "sibbits;" but we have the true stem occurring in the now perverted "gossip" which originally meant a God parent (God sib). Perhaps the most loquacious inhabitants of a parish used most frequently to stand proxy. But although Shakespeare used the word gossip in a bad sense, my Johnson's Dictionary reminds me that Spenser used it in a good one. The term " idiot " has passed through a similar change of meaning. Once implying a private gentleman, it now conveys the idea of one deprived of his reason. Please allow me to thank those who publicly and privately have written me about bird names subsequently to your kindly publishing my list.

M. C. H. BIRD.

As the correspondence now appearing in your columns is very interesting, here are one or two words I have not yet seen mentioned. *Shy-wannicking*; as *wherey yow bin shy-wannicking tew*. Upon inquiring after a person's health, we hear, "Oh, I'm tolerable, kinder arter the ould sort."

A "Norfolk Swimmer."

Kindly allow me space for a word or two anent the *patois* of Norfolk. Once upon a time, as the story books begin, I owned an Irish cob that was a confirmed biter, and on going to see a friend at Reepham I told his factotum of the cob's vicious propensity, but notwithstanding this he attempted to clean him without either putting on a cradle provided or tying him up short. The result was that the old man soon came trembling to my friend, and said, "By *gom*, master, he very nearly *fungered* me."

It strikes me the following is somewhat "broad":—
"I never rid sich a hoss. Well there, bor, he kin go. When we got to the tree acres, where the owd yows are, he was all of a *malt*. There was a heavy *dag* afore breakfast, and *strus* as I'm alive I just felt a *spit* o rain, so I must see arter them woats else our master'll be *nation* riled, and them *calves* 'll be blaring for their wittles as they allus du if they are kep waitin a minit. My missus ha' *scrushed* har little finger good tidily and had to go to the *chemisters* for some stuff, it finely ache and *take on*. T. G. S.

In common with many of your readers, I have been a pleased observer of the correspondence which has taken place in your valuable paper on "Broad Norfolk." Being especially interested in "M. C. H. Bird's" capital contributions, I was somewhat surprised to see the "Scamel" omitted from the list of peculiar names applied to the birds of Norfolk. The sweet bard of Avon makes the lick-spittle Caliban to address the drunken Stephano thus:—

> I prithee let me bring thee where crabs grow,
> And I, with my long nails, will dig thee pig nuts,
> Show thee a jay's nest, and instruct thee how
> To snare the nimble marmozet. I'll bring thee
> To clustring filberts, and sometimes I'll get thee
> Young *scamels* from the rock.

One of our most eminent ornithologists tells us that the gunners of Blakeney, Norfolk, still call a bird of the Godwit type by this name, a fact which I can confirm. An old taxidermist showed me a specimen there some four years ago. Some of Shakespeare's commentators have been dubious in accepting this bird as the one referred to in the text, one of the chief objections being that there are no rocks at Blakeney. The beautiful pebbly beach at this seaport, however, points to there being some substance of a very hard nature in the far off ages, and the number of eggs still laid among stones which are beyond the reach of the waves, and the number of young ones reared would surprise many of your readers.

I venture to express a hope that some handy publication on this subject may be the outcome of this correspondence, in the compiling of which a distinction should be made between words of purely Saxon-cum-Norfolk origin and those phrases which murder the English language. Some of your correspondents have failed to make this distinction.

The following are such good specimens of how Norfolkers can mutilate the Queen's English that I hope you will find room for them. A youth was once asked by his schoolmaster to account for his absence on the preceding day. "It snewed and it blewed and of course I couldn't comed," was the answer. Before the Education Act, in the "good old times," when the endowment of nearly every village school was used for the purposes of secondary education an unnamed pedagogue had, well to put it mildly, the temerity to label his "Dotheboys Hall" as the "Commercial Academy." An old fisherman was struck "all of a haaps" one morning by this notice, and after looking at it for some time to decipher it he was heard to mutter as he jogged along: "Com-i-cal Ak-e-demy: what the dickens is that?" A native who has not been schooled always says "each" for itch. Villagers call a prop a *promp*, the running stream is still called the *beck*, while the island on which the alder grows has itself become the *alder*. I wish to confirm what has already been stated on one side in reference to the term "deek" or "deke." In North Norfolk it is never used to designate a holl or ditch, but refers to the banks of the hedges.

Roughton.   S. E. BAKER.

Our attention has been called to the following letters which appeared in the "Gentleman's Magazine" in 1791:—

MOISE.

It is a common saying amongst the common people in this place (Norwich), when a person does not seem to recruit after a fit of illness, or when he does not thrive in the world, that such an one does not *moise*. Now, sir, I have ransacked several of our English dictionaries, both ancient and modern, but can find no such word, nor indeed any word that this is likely to be a corruption of; and, as I never heard it used anywhere else but here, and can find no one acquainted with its etymology, I thought, perhaps, some of your ingenious correspondents might be able to trace its original; or if not, that it might possibly be an addition to the long catalogue of nondescripts with which Mr. Croft's Dictionary is to abound. M.

The subjoined appeared in reply:—"M," in p. 1022, wishes to know the meaning of "He does not *moise*," a Norfolk phrase when a person does not seem to recruit after a fit of illness, or does not thrive in the world. It appears to be the verb belonging to *moison*, which, with some of its family, is still found in French. *Moison* has been in our language. Chaucer uses it, and Tyrwhitt's "Glossary" explains it, "harvest," "growth,"—Urry's, from Skinner, "ripeness." *Moise—moison*—had the same relation, perhaps, as *grow - growth, succeed—success, &c.*

The dictionary of the gentleman whom "M" mentions is likely to *moise*, I hope; and will, perhaps, go to press this winter with more than 20,000 words which are not in Johnson, supported by authorities. "M" will oblige Mr. C. very much by communicating to your magazine or your printer any other provincial phrases, all of which will turn out, perhaps, not to be corruptions (as "M" supposes *moise*), but the language of our ancestors, and the seeds of our own language. H. C.

N.B.—The dictionary referred to above, which was to have been entitled, "The New Dictionary of the English Language," by the Rev. Herbert Croft, LL.B., London, 1788, was for some reason never published.

I hasten to reply to the Rev. M. C. H. Bird as regards the word *corder*. In my first communication I stated that it appears on notice-boards at Catton. It is in the shape of a warning—" Corder must not be thrown here"—and no doubt is the same as the word *colder*, instanced by Mr. Bird. Dr. Murray, who is editing that magnificent work, the "New English Dictionary," asked me long ago about "corder," and remarked that someone had said it should be *colder*. Professor Furnivall, in 1864, noted the word " corder" on a Norwich notice-board. What is the origin of these words?

Allow me to join with others in the hope that the correspondence on " Broad Norfolk" may be re-published in pamphlet form.

The spelling of the East Anglian dialect words is evidently very unsettled. One of your correspondents writes of a *hawkey*. Bloomfield and others who used the word wrote *horkey*, and I believe Dr. Jessopp writes *baw* instead of the more familiar " bor."

Among Borrow's localisms quoted in my former letter I should have included *lash*. He writes of the grass being " lash and sour."

Rodger's blast, or rodges-blast, is a puzzle. I think the suggested derivation from sirocco is too farfetched. As a fact, does anyone call this windy visitation *Sir Roger?* A possible etymology is from the Anglo-Saxon *rogge*, to shake, used by Chaucer.

With your permission I will add a few more local words:—*Babbing*, a local mode of fishing; *bauleyboats*, Harwich fishing smacks; *boulders*, clumps of flags; *carrs*, low copses in marshes; *dams*, drained marshes; *dydling*, cleaning river bottoms with a scoop; *fleet*, a shallow; *frails*, straw baskets; *gloat*, a species of eel; *hover*, a floating island; *lamming*, bleating of snipe; *liggers*, bundles of reeds to which fishing lines are attached; *loaders*, herring of specially beautiful tints; *miel-banks*, banks of sand blown up by the wind and consolidated by the marum grass—also called " meal-banks"; *pulks*, miniature broads which open off rivers; *putty*, mud on river bottoms, &c.; *quant*, a boating pole—perhaps derived from Latin *contus*, a pole; *rands* or *ronds*, reedcovered banks; *rounding time*, spawning time; *swiping*, raising old anchors for an Admiralty reward; *watereynd*, sea smoke, a dense vapour from the sea.

These examples are all from Mr. Christopher Davies' work on the "Norfolk Broads" (Blackwood, 1884.)

[Other illustrations Mr. Christopher Davies has mentioned to me:—When a marsh is covered with water it is said to be *bright*; a lead pencil is usually called a *cedar* pencil.—C-H.]

I have asked in vain for an explanation of the word *coquilles*, which Mr. Rye, in his "History of Norfolk," calls "our Norwich *coquail*." I do not know his authority for this strange spelling. It may be connected with cockell bread, or kichell cakes. The latter were given by godfathers and godmothers whenever their godchildren sought a blessing from them. Perhaps when godchildren ceased to ask for these blessings, kichell cakes also became obsolete.

The word *scamel* has a special interest from Shakspeare's use of it. Not long since there was a leaderette on the subject in the *Daily News*, which I cut out, but cannot now find.

I fear the interest of the subject is leading me to an inordinate trespass on your hospitable columns, but I should just like to state that the Greek word from which we derive idiot was not specially applied to gentlefolks, but rather to the "dim common populations," for, no doubt as Mr. Bird is aware, our earliest versions of the Bible have "the idiotes heard him gladly"—*i.e.*, the common people, a Greek idiot being any private, ordinary person, having no official status. Just as the common people became idiots, so did the holy people become silly—*selig*, holy, and as the dire Gehenna, the ever-burning rubbish heap outside Jerusalem, has dwindled amongst infidel Frenchmen into *gêne*, a bore!

I don't know why *muck* should be claimed as a native word of these parts. Lord Verulam, sometimes wrongly called Lord Bacon, said "Money is like muck, not good except it be spread." HET VARKE.

Before closing the interesting correspondence on this subject I should like, with your permission, to make one or two suggestions. The Rev. M. C. H. Bird and Mr. A. Patterson having given us the local nicknames by which the feathered tribes of East Anglia are known, would it not be equally interesting if some one would do the like for the weeds and wild flowers, trees, and shrubs of the same district? In the building trade amongst labourers and artisans a great number of local terms are used which are not found in any architectural dictionary such as *Jimmies* or *Jimmers* for hinges, *Pamments* for pavement tiles, *colder* for brick rubbish, &c. A list of all which provincialisms would be very valuable.

The suggestion to reprint these contributions in book form is good; but to be of use they should all be recast in alphabetical order, and at the same time it would be as well to annotate the present collection with Halliday, Moor, Faby, Nall, Isaac Taylor, and the "East Anglian Notes and Queries," which last contains a great number of provincialisms not be found elsewhere.

Every district and county in England has its peculiar dialect, though making use of many words which are common to several, or even all; but with the School Board in full operation everywhere they will probably in the course of a generation or so entirely disappear and be lost. This would be a great pity, and therefore before such a catastrophe takes place, would it not be well for the leading daily paper in each county to open its columns for correspondence on the subject, and so make collections similar to the one you are now making, which will be priceless hereafter.

How this is to be brought about I do not know. Possibly the "Philological," "Folk Lore," or other societies might see their way to undertake it; but it appears to me it should be done through the newspapers, and not by the different archæological journals. Their circulation is not sufficient, and they do not reach the class which would be likely to forward the matter. Every one takes the newspaper, and the response which has been made since " C-H." first threw down the gauntlet on the last day of last year has been simply astonishing, one feels wholly *stammed* to find such a large body of information forthcoming in so short a time. No less than 91 letters from 75 different writers have appeared from December 31st, 1892, to January 18th, 1893, inclua period of nineteen days only! It is worth while contrasting this with the *twenty years* gatherings of a local archæological journal upon the same subject simply to show—without any disparagement whatever to the journal—the superior collective power of the daily Press, its extensive publicity and far-reaching ramifications. The "East Anglian Notes and Queries," commenced in 1858 by by the late Mr. Samuel Tymms, F.S.A., and continued to the time of his lamented decease in 1870, recommenced in 1885 by the Rev. Evelyn White, and continuing to the present time, has only published fifty-nine communications from forty-five writers upon this subject, and very many of these letters have been discussions upon single words only. It will, therefore, be seen at once the superior agency of the daily Press in forwarding this work all over the kingdom, and to be of use it should be done at once.

I was sorry to see the letter of your correspondent "L. J." in this morning's issue. It is the only jarring note that has been heard, and is calculated to damp others. "L. J.," if not bilious, is unreasonable. He should remember that a newspaper is like a fishing net —it gathers everything. The fisherman does not reject the whole of his "Laul" because it contains some "*rubbidge*," he very wisely separates the one from the other — as the farmer does " the wheat from the tares" and the " sheep from the goats." Let him listen to the Rev. Isaac Taylor, " Nineteen-twentieths of the vocabulary of any people lives only in the literature and the speech of the cultured classes. But the remainder—the twentieth part—has a robust life in the daily usage of the sons of toil, and this limited portion of the national speech never fails to include the names of those objects which are the most familiar and the most beloved.

JOHN L. CLEMENCE.

I have been much interested in the articles and correspondence in your paper concerning provincial words more or less peculiar to the Norfolk dialect, and if not too late I should like to mention an incident from my own experience. A fisherman on Cromer Beach once remarked in the course of a conversation " The sea is a *smoultin* now." and further explained this by saying that " it gits kinder smoother when the tide is goin' out." It is a well known fact that in stormy weather the sea becomes calmer during the ebb tide, and " smoultin " appears to be the colloquial expression on the Norfolk coast which describes this phenomenon. ARTHUR W. WISEMAN.

Now we ha got our 'lotments we can grow greens, grains, and taters, and roisberries and guseberries tu, which is suffin new ; and a good help 'tis to find wittles for our housen. Besides, now larning is *gan* in, and since wages is hained to what they warr a few year back—when Joe Arch axt us all to jine the Union and pull straight—we ought, afore long, to be a heap better tu do than the old uns wore, who had to live on dry brade. They wore nowhere then—no wage, no 'lotments, no edication. Just you come and pake round my 'lotment and see my nuvering (manœuvring), and I will show you what the lond will grow. I ha got a rum funny lot of taters ; they are some bigness, and rare good ating into the bargin ; besides parsnips and carrots and the like, which help to stop a gap where you have a lot of kids to find wittels for. I keep a pig in the sty now, John bor, and he ate up all the *cayed* taters and other refuge that we het to grow that would be 'stried. Lately my missus have been tending him on male and fine brun, and being a good grubber is right fit for the knife ; which (hold your whip) will come in for rent, which hev allus been a puzzler for us iver since we heb been spliced. What do make me so fidgety when the gals and chaps fall out is that they soon get from words to blows about nothing. There is such a duller made with them mawthers. You can hear them blubbering, blaring, and mobben, when I het to go arter them and square em all, they du fare such duzzy fules. I say, together, you ha got what a good many hant, a place to antic in. You can all muse yarselfs and play tit a mȧ torter, and hub ma grub, and the likes. Therefore sattle down and let us hear no more of your squalling and squaking. An Arch Labourer.

"Het Varke" and other correspondents have pointed out how difficult is the orthography of dialectic pronunciation. This accounts for "corder," "colder," &c. A few such instances occur in the words quoted by "Het Varke" from Mr. Davies' "Norfolk Broads." *Frails* I have always heard of as "Flail baskets ;" the former gives the meaning but the latter is the provincial term. *Gloat* becomes "glotts" or "glutts." *Hove* should be "hover" or "huvver."

Miel banks is never used in E. Norfolk, but always "hills" or "sandhills." *Quant* approaches its Latin equivalent more nearly when pronounced, as it sometimes is, "quont." Although the rudd are here called roud, yet all Broadland fishes are said to be on the roud (not round) when spawning. I did not intend to use "gentleman" in its present restricted sense, in my last communication, as the latter part of the sentence in which it occurred shows, for both a gentleman and a scavenger are equally liable to lose their reason. Even this "gentleman" has a better provincial meaning than is usually conveyed by the term. Here it means "generous," not necessarily "one as lives right up," but "you're a gentleman" means you're a real one. Whenever I have heard the Broadland sirocco spoken of it has always been as "Sir Rodger." Perhaps it happened thus :—A boatman might have heard a yachting gent say, "Why, that was a regular sirocco." There is no doubt that many modern Norfolk words are corruptions from some such repetitions and hurried readings. The present correspondence is very useful, because it shows what words are now in use, and several almost obsolete, "plancher" and "goaf," *e.g.*, have been brought to light and life. Mr. Clemence made a good suggestion when he said that individuals should become specialists, and make separate collections of terms used in special branches of—what shall I say—"work and play." A builder's list would have given us colder, and a coleopterist's collection should contain a "Bishop-Barnabee" (Bishop pronounced Bisher). With the same idea in my head I wrote to Mr. Patterson to give us a catalogue of piscatorial nick-names. These he sent to me instead of to you, as I suggested, thinking in his native modesty that they would not be sufficiently interesting for publication. Marshall's "Rural Economy" (1795) contains some 300 provincialisms connected with agriculture, collected by himself in two years. It was more easy for him to "spot" such things then, for he was a stranger amongst us, whereas we who have been accustomed to hear these words and phrases from our youth up fail to notice some of them. Moreover, there was not so much "slang" in those days, nor had books, papers, and railways reduced the mother tongue to such a dead level as now. "Herbert Andrews" calls homebrew "arms and legs." I once heard something like it applied to the much maligned, but muchly imbibed, brewer's " stuff." Upon asking at a village pub. for some of their " best and mildest " to take on to the broad, a man in the bar said " *Tangle leg*, you mean." " What do you mean by tangle leg ? " said I. " Oh, what get inter yer legs, and make yer legs fly about afore it get inter yer heead," says he. We have a curious custom surviving in this little village, that of the children going round and hollering (singing) " Good Morrer, Walentin," in expectation of some trifling recognition of their good wishes, which in order to perpetuate the harmless amusement I make a point of reciprocating. What is the origin of the children of Horning hollerin, " Ho John Barleycorn " to river passengers ? Does any such custom prevail elsewhere ? I wonder no reference has been made to superstitions, charms, and witchery, but I must desist or I shall have some bodies, " Sprites " perhaps, " over-looking " me to-morrow.

M. C. H. BIRD.

P.S.—I was glad to see this morning in the *Eastern Daily Press* that a suggestion of mine was likely to be acted upon, viz., that the local Mutual Improvement Society might with pleasure and profit discuss Broad Norfolk. Will "An Arch Labourer" tell us how he plays " hub ma grub ? "

I venture to trouble you with a few words which I have been accustomed to hear in common use. I think they are fresh to your interesting collection. I should like also to see a collection of Norfolk sayings and superstitions.

Beetle, a wooden mallett used with wedges to "rive" up timber ; *baulks*, ridges for sowing mangold ; *bile*, the bale or handle of a pail ; *betsy*, a teakettle ; *barm*, yeast or leaven, beer tasting of " yist " is " barmy ; " *barmy*, a soft person, a " Susan ; " *brumble*, bramble or blackberry bush.

Cosh, the chaff or husk of wheat, also a stick; *chummy*, a sparrow and a soft felt hat ; *clates*, heel irons on boots ; *cobble*, the stone of fruit, lime, and paving-stones ; *church-hole*, a grave, a term used to frighten children.

Doss or *Dossett*, a hassock for kneeling upon; *dump*, a term in brickmaking, a short, fat person is called "a little dump;" *daft*, demented; *dibbling*, using dibbles for "corn droppers," mostly done by women walking backward; *dumplin dust*, flour.

Faut for fault; *full flopper*, a full-fledged nestling; *flight of bees*, a swarm, not being the first one from the hive.

Hod, as coal hod, brick hod, mangold hod, *etc.*; *hotch-potch*, Irish stew (also a legal term); *hind*, a term of reproach, a scoundrel.

Jill, a two-wheeled carriage for timber, one with four wheels is a *drug*; *jot*, part of the inside anatomy of a pig.

Lucum, a garret window.

Pollard, a tree that has been "topped and lopped;" *posset*, a mixture of treacle and milk for a cough

Quick-set, young white thorn-plants.

Rafe-boards, on wagons; also applied to high shirt collars; *run*, a brook of water.

Scrog, to cut field beans with a sickle or hook; *shanks's pony*, one's own legs; *shepherd's flock*, white fleecy clouds, indicative of fine weather; *Sally*, a hare; *settle*, a high-backed seat used in inns.

Ting, to beat a shovel with a key when bees swarm; *tupp*, a ram; *tang*, the tongue of a buckle or "Jew's harp;" *top-sawyer*, "the boss;" *toad-in-the-hole*, a batter pudding baked with a piece of meat in it.

Wap, flog or "trounce."

E. SKINNER.

"Moise" I have frequently heard used by nonscoring partners at whist or bowls. One will remark, "We don't seem to 'moise,' partner." *Snatchet* is a word I have heard frequently when somebody has done what he thought a clever thing, but got defeated in his object. "You thought you had done a snachet." It seems to refer to some kind of sharp practice. I hear occasionally dentists referred to as *gum ticklers*, and organists as *wind jammers*, but are these terms confined to Norfolk?

EDWARD T. AYERS.

It is with no small interest that I have read the numerous letters on "Broad Norfolk." Although so large a number of words and sayings have been inserted in your columns, I believe the following have up till now been omitted. The word *doss* (meaning a hassock), and *bunny* (a swelling caused by a blow on the head), as well as *cussy* for a rap on the hand, are all pure Norfolk words. Then there are expressions such as ; "There mor doan't stand ther' star garping at me, but go inter shud and git the biler, and doan't forgit to bring the leed, and look here, bor, if yow *twilt* him I'll twilt yow, so mind yer that." The latter expression I heard (no later than last month) used by an old lady to a boy who had been "twilting" (fighting) her grandson. DAISY DIMPLE.

I should like to tell you I have seen the *feeten* of an old hin amun the *pelanders* (polyanthus), and to drive her out of the garden have said *Hush, Huush,* many times. Is not "Huush" another form of "Woosh"—go from me? L. A. BUSSEY.

I have read most of the correspondence in your paper respecting "Broad Norfolk." The majority of the words dealt with I have heard spoken in that part of Norfolk which lies between Wroxham and North Walsham. A *bannock* is a word in common use, meaning a cake baked in a French oven. When a labourer has had one of these for his morning meal he *twidges* off to work on the farm. If the man is a stupid fellow he is called by his comrades a *"duke's* headed fulo;" if he is occasionally the worse for drink, and not to be depended upon, they say he has no *persayrance* over *hisself*. I have heard this word used hundreds of times in the parish of Tunstead, Norfolk. W. W.

I am glad to hear that the highly entertaining correspondence on this subject is to be gathered together in a pamphlet. Such a volume will form a really valuable Norfolk dictionary, and must prove curious and interesting to many in city and county.

May I be allowed to add one or two strange localisms which have escaped notice hitherto?

In many parts of the county the phrase, "That'll hull him in a buffle," is often heard, which, being interpreted is, "That'll put him in a difficulty, or a bother."

When the crescent moon is in a certain position it is said " the mune lays *water-shutin*'." As soon as it has passed "full" it is said to be *on the dreep*.

Some in the country districts will perhaps remember that ripe gooseberry pie is known as *thape pie*.

F. G. S.

In perusing an edition of the *Staffordshire Advertiser* of March, 1815, I found several words differently spelt, as—"Smoak" for smoke, "compleat" for complete, "chuse" for chose, "tythe" for tithe, "chissel" for chisel. A gun was advertised as a "fowling piece." Another paragraph contained "And tools of every 'denomination.'" A man was advertised as a draper, mercer, dealer, and *chapman*; also another, including, "three cows, three *twinters*, and two calves." Can anyone please inform me what is meant by "chapman" and "twinter." The plural of shoe was *shoeses*, as in :—" My wife and myself and the muses, with forty-five pair of new *shoeses*." Can anyone please inform me where "Cockey Lane," in which Brown & Barker were hatmakers, was in Norwich, as published in an old publication of the *Norfolk Chronicle*, November, 1809.

W. L.

The following words and expressions occur to me at the present moment as being peculiar to Norfolk:—*Jot*, a heavy article of any description; *tremble*, pork cheese; *limpsy*, loose, flabby; *vardle*, bottom hinge of a gate. The famous Stiffkey cockles are always called "Stukey Blues."

HERBERT ANDREWS.

If your correspondent "W. L." had been in the habit of reading old books he would know that compleat, smoak, and tythe were quite correct spellings not long ago. It is a great pity that more people do not read Chaucer and Spenser, in whose writings they would find plentiful examples of common words in their infancy. Chapman, a merchant or trader, is of very common use in Chaucer, and by no means uncommon to this day. Borrow uses the word in " The Gypsies of Spain," 1872, page 137.

" Twinters " is an abbreviation of two-winters, and means cattle two winters old.

Breck districts are, I think, only so described in the Eastern Counties. There is a full account of them in Stevenson's " Birds of Norfolk, Vol. I.," Introduction p. 6.

Gaggles and *skeins* of geese are referred to in vol. iii. of that work; no doubt Mr. Southwell can say if they are local terms. From the same work I learn that when swans have nested the marshmen say that they have *timbered*.

Whether *Cob* and *Pen*, for the cock and hen swan are local words or not I cannot say.

The word *susserara*, or *sisserara*, I believe occurs in the " Vicar of Wakefield," and has proved a hard nut. It *may* be connected with poor Sisera's experience, but the derivation is unlikely. The *sound* reminds one of the Latin *sussurrus*, a whispering.

To answer Mr. Bird's inquiry as to saying " God bless you " to a person who sneezes would take me far afield. The custom is general all the world over. Years ago in the wilds of Brazil I hardly ever heard a person sneeze without the ready exclamation from the bystanders, " *Dios guarda vossa merced!* "—God preserve you! A legend on the subject was that one of the Popes was choked and died through sneezing, hence the prayer. But the custom dates back far beyond Popes. There is an instructive article on the subject in " The Comet " for the 14th inst. HET VARKE.

Since my letter of the 20th I have thought of a few more words (contained in the following) which are peculiar to the people of Norfolk:—
"Hallo, narbor, yow look kinder riled this mornin'. Wo's up wi' yer?" "Bor, I'm nearly off my nut. That old sweep ha' been here to fye my *chimbly* out, and I'm blow'd if he haint *funked* the sut all over the place. The *backstork* (back stove) is chock full, and my backus is smuddered wi't, and if that ain't enough to make a parson swear I don't know what is, du

yow?" The word stuttering is called *hackering*, and hands are termed *dannies* in such sentences as "Tha's right, me little darlin', clap your dannies;" and I may add in closing that by very "broad Norfolkers" an umbrella is a *dickey-shud*.   DAISY DIMPLE.

I have been trying to remember Norfolk phrases not hitherto mentioned by your correspondents, but, alas! my memory fails me. However, I do not think the following peculiarities have yet been noticed:—

"Without a *chance*," for "without a doubt."
"*Like* to be," for "likely to be."
"I'm *hampered* to *get hold* of my breath," for "I find it difficult to breathe."
"*Fatagued*," for "annoyed."
"*Right consistent*" to do something, for "quite determined."
"*Can't-a-bide*," for "dislike."
"*Pick-cheese*," for "tomtit."

Many of the Norfolk gentry talk "Norfolk" quite unwittingly, and can easily be recognised by other Norfolk persons in all parts of the world.   RECTOR.

Perhaps I am late in the field to give one or two expressions which have occurred to me while travelling in various parts of Norfolk on the iron steed. I have been asked, "Isn't it rough travelling *abroad*, master?" Frequently "abroad" is spoken only to mean outside. We have been directed to keep straight on till you come to a *heater*, and take the road to right or left, according to where we were bound for, a heater meaning where two roads meet, forming the apex of a triangle. Many other phrases crop up to the observant cyclist, and words which to many are quite foreign in meaning.   W. A. HOTSON.

Look yow here, bor, don't yow maller wut; if yow get a pint of allers inter yow, yow don't know how to fare. If yow want a thackin or a smack o' the chaps dew yow dut.   S. J. W.

In the "vulgar tongue," to change one's linen is to "shiffen oneself." Many years ago a curate-in-charge was appointed to a parish where I myself had been formerly curate. He was the first clergyman of that parish who had ever preached in his surplice. One day, when driving through the parish, I called upon a singular old couple, who used to be constant attendants at the church in my day. Quoth the old man, "Du you know our new pareson, sir?" On my answering in the affirmative, he replied, "Wall, for a *dark* man, he is the prettiest little man I ever see in my life." My friend was evidently not an admirer of *dark* men.

The old lady now chimed in, and said in a confidential tone, "Du yow know, he never *shiffen hisself* all thro' the sarvice," by which she meant me to understand that he preached in his surplice, and did not substitute a black gown for a white one. CLERICUS.

At the risk of being called *bilious or unreasonable* by your correspondent "John L. Clemence," I must say that to a large extent I agree with "L. J." that a lot of nonsense has crept into this Broad Norfolk correspondence. I take it, sir, that your original intention in starting the correspondence was to rescue from oblivion certain archaic words and phrases that are fast disappearing from the vocabulary of the county, and also if possible to ascertain their derivation. Many of the letters you have published contain little else than mispronounced or misused words:— "Harbert" for Herbert, "labarneum" for laburnum, the use of "contain" for detain, "deficient" for sufficient, &c. What these and such as these can have to do with "Broad Norfolk" I cannot see, and I trust when you bring out your glossary you will eliminate all such words, and, as I before suggested, submit the list to a competent tribunal of old Norfolkers before publication. I am quite sure when it does come out it will be a most interesting compilation, and will be eagerly sought after by many.

Tree is the common pronunciation of "three," but surely no one ever heard of "tree threes" for three trees.

Skinker is a capital old word still used in this district. I should very much like to know its root.

Sneck, a door latch is in common use here, but I question whether it is distinctively Norfolk; an old dictionary gives it as Scotch.

Dead-a-bird, with an indescribable pronunciation of the last word—something between "bird" and "bud"—was in common use when I was a boy, meaning nearly dead or dying.

Daisy Dimple's, "twilt," is a good specimen of Broad Norfolk.   OLD NORFOLK.

Allow me to add a few words to the list of Norfolkisms which have already appeared in your columns.

A *spline, i.e.,* a thin strip of wood.
A *lower,* used for a lever.
Rumbustious, used of plants when growing rank.
Living upright, i.e., living on one's means, not having to earn one's living.
Sales, for hames, part of the harness of a horse.
Ped, a hamper.
To have a great *slight* for clothes, *i.e.,* to wear them out very quickly.
To buy a thing *off* a person is also a very common expression.

It is also exceedingly interesting to notice how much more nearly our Norfolk pronounciation of many words approaches the German rather than the English pronounciation when the words are similar in the two languages; instances are—fire, butter, post, pain; to give a person a "dressing" or "troshing," cf. German, dreschen, gedroschen. We have also a few instances of a plural in -n, so common in German, as nezen for nests, housen for houses, meezen for mice. These instances are interesting as showing that the old Saxon language, the language of the Teutons, has not quite died out in England.   P. E. D.

As "Broad Norfolk" is to be republished in a more permanent form, with your permission *explebo numerum* of your correspondents and letters on the subject, *reddesque tenebris.* The following words and quaint local expressions I have not yet seen recorded. *Squackle,* an old parishioner once said to me, on being asked how she was —Well sir, *no matters*, only *pretty middlin,* a tissicking cough has troubled me a good deal, and last night I was nearly *squackled!* (Compare this with " quaggled " under E. Hewett, *Eastern Daily Press*, January 16th.)

Gruttling—" I heard a gruttling (queer noise) up the chimbly."

Swang—" Swang on to him," *i. e.*, give him a good smack.

Slippy—"Look slippy," *i.e.*, be quick. (Is this Norfolk ?)

In *Eastern Daily Press*, January 16th, "Rector" says " Norfolk people are fond of using *long* words, of which they do not know the meaning." Now had he said *fine* words I should have been at one with him, but Norfolkians as well as John Bull in general hate *long* words, and cut them short as they can, as in 'bacca, 'cayed, 'taters, &c. Sometimes they will divide them into two, as chrysanthemums into christmas anthems ; and sometimes in a waggish spirit they will call China asters Chinese oysters. We shorten words much as a Norfolk bucolic tops and tails a turnip, only with this difference:—We are thrifty, and save our tops and tails for use. Thus maw for mawther (as cab for cabriolet), bor (not baw) for neighbour; and so mums for chrysanthemums and 'bus for omnibus.

It certainly seems odd that no explanation or derivation has been found for *wheesh* (or *woosh*) except that which Forbey gives, and he says it *certainly* comes from gauche (left), whereas it means " go to the right." If so the word, like the rule of the road itself, is a paradox.

> The rule of the road is a paradox quite,
> For as you are driving along,
> If you go to the *left* you're sure to go *right*,
> If you go the *right* you go *wrong*.

We have in our language another word *whist*— parallel to *wheesh* and very like it, especially if it is pronounced *wheest*; and for neither of them has any explanation or derivation yet been found. In all probability these words were originally spelt *hweesh* and *hwist*, and this possibly may suggest some solution.

W. F.

The following broad Norfolk words are constantly used in the parish of Tunstead and neighbourhood:—*Traunce*, a great deal of walking to no purpose; *wanklin*, a delicate child; and *bunker*, one who fails to face danger.
W. WATSON.

I fear your very interesting list of Norfolk words will be coming to an end, and am therefore much pleased with the proposal that they are to be printed in a pamphlet. Before the list is concluded I venture to add some words which I believe have not been included.

Slov (from slovenly)—"She did fare to slov." [Yarmouth.]

Popples—For willow trees (from poplar?).

Kider-er—Pork butcher (local).

Doated tree—A dying tree (local).

Has the following expression been given:—"That tree du fare to have a *muddle head*!"
NORTH NORFOLK.

As it seems likely that there may be some permanent outcome of the present correspondence I venture once more to trouble you for the purpose of mentioning one expressive word I do not remember to have been noticed. The word is *popple*. "There, there don't popple"—means don't talk nonsense. To me the word is very suggestive of sound without sense.
E.

As a west countryman, and therefore in Norfolk parlance a "furriner," may I be allowed to mention one or two words that I have not noticed in the correspondence on this subject, viz., *swad*, pork-cheese; *frimmicating* or *frimmocky*, one who is particular as to dress; and *shammock*, a sloven? On the road to Cossey I once asked a labourer what the time of day was, and he informed me, "A little arter tree, and a good deal."
J. L.

In the list of local bird names I said that I could not find a derivation for "mow." I don't know how it was that I did not think of it at the time, but the word is evidently a corruption of "mew," a term of general application to all the smaller gulls, probably from their "cry." The Rev. E. W. Dowell has kindly written me as follows:—"Mag loon" or "lowan" is, I take it, given to the northern diver because of its greater size compared with the red throat, as the large plaice trawled in the North Sea are called mag plaice, when caught among the smaller ones of the harbours and estuaries (query, magnus). There is no surer find for scammells and picks in autumn than the "rocks" (as they are called at Cromer, and "scalps" at Hunstanton), *i.e.*, large stones with sandy water courses between, where small molluscs and crustaceans abound. Andrew Lang asked what Shakespeare meant by "Scammells from the rock" in the *Illustrated London News* a few months ago, and seemed satisfied when I told him of the Norfolk meaning of the word. The gunners used to distinguish the "scammells," that is, the large female godwits from the "picks," the smaller males and young birds." From the above quotation, in which the prefix "mag" is applied to both fish and fowl, there can be little doubt as to the meaning or derivation of the term. The only locality in which I have met with godwits frequently, or in any quantity, was at the mouth of the Thames. There the deep black mud is stoneless, and so the explanation of scammells, as *scar*-mells had not hitherto occurred to me. Moreover, I thought that Caliban's words referred to some birds *bred*, upon the rocks, and therefore thought, as Mr. Southwell suggested and many footnotes to the passage have explained, that "sca" was a misprint for "sea." There yet remains the "mell" to be derived. Forby gives "mell" to swing or wheel round, to turn anything slowly about, from resemblance to the motion of a mill. Such "tumbling" or headlong flight would be more applicable to the dipping and shailing of gulls than the far steadier flight of godwits.

When helping a man to "shove" a punt along the ice into a "wake" one day last week he exclaimed, whilst resting a moment to get wind, "This here is fit to malt yar blood," *malt* or *molt* being the provincial for perspiration, a mere corruption of melt; in fact, we speak correctly when we talk of molten lead. On January 19th Mr. Wiseman wrote,

"The sea is smoultin' now," that is, melting away, only "smouldering" after passing through the process of "smelting" during the storm. "Wake" as used above is an open piece of water in the midst of a broad, the remaining surface of which is "laid" or frozen over. "Wak" is the Norwegian term for the same. (Lloyd's "Game Birds and Wildfowl").—

M. C. H. BIRD.

P. S.—Harting in his Ornithology of Shakespeare quotes the passage from *Tempest*, Act II., Scene 2, as

"Sometimes I'll get thee
Young *sea-mells* from the rock."

He remarks: "It is evident that the sea-mell, sea-mew, or sea-gull is intended, the young birds being taken before they could fly." Harting does not so much as suggest that *scamels* was the reading of the Old copy. Johnson suffered *scamels* to stand because, as he tells us, somebody had observed that limpets are in some places called *scams*.

Here are still a few more words :—

Dardledumdue—A person without energy or knack. "She's a poor dardledumdue."

Sidewiper—A blow on the side of anything with a stick. "I gave her such a side-wiper."

Pilcochia—A thrashing. "I gave him pilcochia."

Dakes-headed—"You great dakes-headed thing."

Slussy-hound—One fond of drink.

Gaddy-wentin'—Gossiping.

Flareup—A row.

The compiler of the coming pamphlet cannot do better than consult three or four agricultural labourers, and I hope he will ask them particularly whether they know a deke from a holl, as one writer maintained that a deke was a holl! I quite agree with all "Old Norfolk" says in your Monday's paper.

NORFOLK DUMPLING.

Before you close the interesting correspondence on Norfolk words will you allow me to give one, which I do not think has already appeared, *i.e.*, "*wittery*," meaning weak, frail. A feeble puny child

I have heard described thus, and also as a "witterer." I have never seen the word written, so can only spell it phonetically.
C.

Kindly allow me to add a few words to your very interesting correspondence on "Broad Norfolk," which, after all, is not more broad than Lincolnshire, where they speak of girls as "wenches." The other day I overheard the following:—" Chuck a snowball inter owd Biller;" to which Billy replied, " Bor, yow batter nut dut, du *I'll woller yer.*
MOLLIE.

I see that your correspondent "C. H. Bird" suggests that the term Sir Roger, as applied to the squalls which are encountered in Broadland, may have had for its origin possibly some remark addressed by a yachting gentleman to his subordinate describing one of the squalls as a " sirocco," and which the aforesaid subordinate perhaps laid hold of as Sir Roger. But long before the yachting gentleman ever aired his resplendent rig out or his siroccos in the presence of a gaping and prehensile waterman, these heavy gusts of wind were called Sir Roger's blasts. The sudden and mysterious manner in which (on an otherwise perfectly still and calm day in summer) they come sweeping and whistling over the reed and sedge clad country, bending the rushes to the surface of the water as if compelling their proud and feathery heads by one rough blow to make obeisance, filled the heart of the lonely countryman in days gone by with superstitious fear. Not because some wiseacre had alluded to them as "siroccos," which in itself would be calculated to cause sensations of alarm in the mind of the average marshman : but because tradition had handed down to him that the icy breath of the restless spirit of Sir Roger Ascham fanned his cheek, causing him to tremble like one who (according to his superstitious notions) shudders only as he steps across his own grave. Details of the legend I am unable to give, having forgotten them ; and the work on Folk Lore of Norfolk, which I take as my authority for the origin of the appellation of " Roger's blast," has unfortunately been mislaid.

I have not noticed amongst the words already given as peculiar to Norfolk, the word *pit* for pond. A youth invariably requests the pleasure of the company of a friend at a select sliding party by couching his invitation in the following graceful language:—" C'e on booy les we goo on't pit."

I am not aware whether the omission of the final " s " in the third person singular, present tense, is confined to Norfolk and Suffolk, but it certainly is more marked in these two counties. As examples, perhaps the following will be sufficient to explain " He hev," " he do," " she say." The last is the most common of all, and the odds are very heavy indeed against anyone passing or overtaking a bevy of factory girls without overhearing them (chiefly by the reiteration of the three words " soo she say ") pulling to pieces, after the manner of all womankind, some lady of their acquaintance, who has apparently, from the fragments of invective that you catch, been guilty of piracy in her conquests.

There is no doubt that the Norfolk labourer has his full share of original wit, as anyone will discover who discourses with him. Moreover, there is also some mysterious fountain head of standard wit from which each one in the county draws his supply of repartee, and with which each is fully equipped. The efficiency and universality of this was distinctly proven by a cleric who ventured to indulge in a political discussion with certain knights of the most ancient and honourable order of the ploughshare. The first one was polite enough until he suspected that some expressions beyond " his know " were introduced with the object of enticing him out of his depth ; then he speedily payed out his cable and let go his sheet anchor, retiring from the contest by remarking, in measured tones, " Howsomdever my politics is, and yerl excoose me, but I allus say les hev more pigs and less parsons." This had such a chilling effect on the ecclesiastical politician that he did not feel sufficiently recovered to resume his interviews arriving in the next parish, and even then he deemed it expedient to approach "number two " with caution, liberally served up with melted butter. " Well, my good man "—(every man below a certain status in society a parson considers to be strictly his own property)—" Well, my good man ; it's very fine weather for your work." "Thas jest wer yere wrong, bor; cum, and yew try it, and see if that aint a goin to hull yer in a muck wash!" Such familiarity portended evil, and the ecclesiastic wished himself out of it. A fleeting smile of a sickly nature o'erspread his features, and he resolved to make one more attempt.

"Well, my good man," the reverend gentleman essayed again, with a very third-rate attempt to combine conciliation, pleasantry, and banter in one, "I'm sure a fine, healthy, strong fellow like you has no distorted views on politics. You'll go and vote for the right candidate to-night, won't you?" Never try to draw an agricultural labourer by flattery or banter. Before you can wink the other eye he twigs what you're up to. Straightway came the answer back. No, 'twas not Excelsior, but "Gorstreuth, hold ye yer slaver dew, my politics is, and yerl excoose me"—but that was all—his audience having vanished, his politics were not revealed, although they may perhaps be guessed at.

This preference which the toiler on the land shows for the porcine race over the clergy accounts in a great measure for the "lapsed masses," so far as rural districts are concerned.

Slaver is applied to any mode of speech which may be of a soapy nature, or any continued nagging which may be considered to require a copious flow of saliva to support its protracted delivery. TLICEC.

In the interesting correspondence in your columns, I believe reference has not been made to a peculiar characteristic of the Norfolk peasant, which at once strikes a stranger to the county, namely, the apparent inability to give a decided "Yea, yea," or "Nay, nay." The true Norfolkian commits himself to nothing. There are three answers I received to the question, "Do you think it will rain to-day?" "I don't know as it won't." "It ma'ay and it mayn't." "I don't know but it will." I am a native of Somerset, and have been much amused to hear that county (with others) habitually alluded to as "The Shires," and the dwellers therein as foreigners. Why are all Norfolk verbs in the singular number only? The phrases, "I like myself," and "I made a purposed journey," strike on the foreigner's ear as being quaint, but they explain themselves. Has *botty*, meaning impertinent, been given? E. S. B.

Although not Norfolk or Suffolk born, I have spent the greater portion of my life in East Anglia—first in Suffolk, and later in South Norfolk, where I heard words unfamiliar to me while living in Suffolk. Some of these have been referred to in the "Broad Norfolk" correspondence, viz., *mardle, hutkin, draunt.*

A servant astonished me one day by the following:— "I saa, 'm, I'a had a rare fye out on that back staircase (now unused) and there was a load o' spiders." A Suffolk servant once scared her mistress with "O, ma'm, you're got a great *crock* on yer face." Her mistress—a Norfolk woman—had never heard the word, and in a fright, thinking it was some noxious creature, begged the girl to take it off. It was a "smut" from the kitchen stove.

In a Methodist chapel some years since a good old local preacher of the labouring class said in the course of his sermon, "Dare frinds, ef ye arn't learned in the skule o' Christ ye might as well be fules." I heard this myself, and it made a lasting impression upon me. I have been much interested in "Broad Norfolk," and trust it may be published in permanent form.

S. E. A.

Seal of the day I have always thought a rather poetical expression; it is applied to the greeting of a casual acquaintance "Do you know so-and-so, John? Is he a friend of yours?" "Wall, sir, he ain't much of a frind; but I give him the 'seal of the day' when I meet him."

The word *ridiculous* is used in the sense of shameful. "I never heerd of such conduct. I call it right down ridiculous."

The coroner is, of course, called the "crowner." A man named King died rather suddenly. The villagers were perplexed as to whether the coroner ought to be sent for, or not. One of them went to a Guardian with the remark, "Old King be dade, and we are all on the *averdupois* (uncertain in our minds) as to whether he ought to be 'crowned' or no."

‡ *Crush* is Norfolk for gristle.

Mocking the Church is a curious expression. The villagers have an idea that if after the banns of marriage have been duly published the couple refuse to be married they must pay a fine for "mocking the church."

Pensey, fretful; applied to children. Ah! the child ain't well; she is a poor "pensey little thing."

Clung is an almost untranslatable word. A shrivelled apple is not *tough*; it is *clung*. To my mind no other word conveys the exact meaning of "clung."

The word *respectable* is used not so much in the sense of worthy of respect as to convey the idea that the person to whom the epithet is applied is a little superior in position or circumstances to the speaker. A man who had recently been released from Norwich Castle, once said to me that I should be surprised if I could see how many *respectable* people there were among the criminals.

"Some du say so; *other some* don't." In Acts xvii, 18, we read, "And some said, what will this babbler say? *other some*, he seemeth to be a setter forth of strange gods."

I would say, in conclusion, that, although a stranger, after a few years' residence in the county, would have no difficulty in understanding the Norfolk dialect, he would never *speak* it like a native. As a Norfolk man, bred and born, I think that I have accomplished that art, or perhaps it comes to me naturally. Doubtless, when I am often least conscious of the fact, my speech betrays me. CLERICUS.

Here are a few more Norfolkisms:—

Boke, the body of a wagon or cart.
Dabster, an adept, good hand.
Hobby-lantern, a "Will-o'-the-Wisp."
Fan, a large basket for holding corn, used on a threshing floor.
Mew or muir heart, faint hearted.
Nag, to "jaw."
Numm chance, a speechless stupid.
Riddle, a sieve.
Rockstaff, a tale, "an old woman's rockstaff."
Stub, to grub up tree roots.
Wamp, to splice, as on a boot.   E. S.

I send you a few sundry and fishy items used hereabouts. The weasel is called a *mouse-hunter*; the stoat is a *foumart;* porpoise, a *sea-pig*. In fishing lore a *teller* is a counter; a *shot* net is one when put overboard; *waist*, side of a vessel; *warp*, a rope; *warp* of herring, four in number; *stuff*, herring, e.g., "salt stuff," &c.; *swill*, a herring basket holding 500 herring; *maund*, a basket into which the herring are counted: holds 100; a *long-tale* hundred is really 132; a *last* of herring, 13,200; *fish-house*, curing-house; *spit*, a stick containing 25 herring; *cob*, a pile of herring; *cob*, a roe herring; *horse*, rack on which spits of herring hang to drain; *struck*, the passing down of cured herring; *kipper*, a split smoked herring.

The above terms are but a few of those used in connection with the herring fishery. A. P.

I have not seen in your correspondence upon above the word *bullverin* (cumbersome) nor *rootling* (burrowing), as for example, "A rat has been rootling in the garden." T. G. S.

It has been said that, prior to the advent of the School Board, among the poorer folk of East Norfolk a vocabulary of from 800 to 1000 words formed their entire range of speech. Possibly this may be a correct estimate, and, if so, it is easy to understand why their speech was difficult to be understood by persons not acquainted with the dialect, as probably one-third of their words were either provincial words or the ordinary dictionary words disguised with such a brogue as to be unrecognisable in the singular accent of the natives. Persons who happen to live for a year or two in almost any part of England can acquire the emphasis, accent, and inflection of the dialect of the district, but there is something so extremely puzzling with our Norfolk brogue that but few can imitate it with any degree of accuracy. Actors whose faculty for mimicry is frequently their strong point can imitate the burr of the north-countryman, the brogue of the Irishman, the *patois* of the Scotchman, and the phrasing of the Cornish-man, but I have never yet heard one who could successfully carry on a conversation in the East Norfolk dialect. Their attempts were usually very feeble and transparent, they may use Norfolk *words* but there is something in the mode of *delivery* that is the birthright and heir-loom of the native-born man alone.

Another notable point to be observed is the persistency with which their accent and way of speaking clings to them through life. I have often spoken to men who have been in London twenty, thirty, and even forty years, but a very few sentences will serve to proclaim the county of their birth. Some men will forget the local words of their childhood (so far as never using them in their coversation), but the Norfolk way of pronouncing attaches itself to the *ordinary* words of speech they use, and so betrays them.

I notice that several of your correspondents have been very busy in compiling a list of birds with their Norfolk names; may I add as an addenda a few Norfolk names of various herbs, shrubs, &c.

Buddle—Corn marigold.
Cankerweed—Common ragwort.
Clote—Coltsfoot.
Cocksheads—Plantain ribwort or ribgrass.
Dindles—Corn or sow thistles.
Gargut Root—Bear's-foot.
Gladdon—Large and small catstail.
Goose Tansey—Silverweed.
Hogweed—Knotgrass.
Muck Weed or Fat-hen—Common goosefoot.
Needleweed—Shepherd's needle.
Owl's Crown—Wood cudweed.
Pickpurse or Sandweed—Common spurry.
Quicks—Couch grass.
Redweed—Round smooth-headed poppy.
Smartweed—Biting and pale-flowered persicarias.
Suckling—White clover.
Winterweed—Ivy-leaved speedwell.
Wret (or Wart) weed—Sun spurge.

ERNEST R. SUFFLING.

A writer in the *Literary World*, under the signature of "T. Le M.D.," refers in learned and appreciative style to the "Broad Norfolk" correspondence recently published in the columns of the *Eastern Daily Press*. He remarks:—

"The popularity of the Norfolk Broads as a delightful holiday resort has recently, by some mental association, turned the attention of the people of the county to their own 'Broad-Norfolk' variety of English; and the *Norfolk News* has wisely opened its pages to any and all who are able to contribute to the knowledge of the dialect. In the number of that journal now before us nearly six columns are occupied by contributions, comprising towards thirty letters, a poem, and two set articles, one of the two being by the author of 'Giles's Trip to London.' It is impossible not to be struck with the interest in their subject shown by the contributors, and with their zealous eagerness to add to the general stock of knowledge. As outsiders it would ill become us to go poaching upon their preserves, or to appropriate their collected spoil, although they can scarcely value it more highly than ourselves. In case, however, our public spirited contemporary should contemplate issuing a '*Norfolk News* Glossary,' or any other collection of East Anglicisms, we will offer one or two brief critical remarks upon points that struck us as we read along.

"And, firstly, the local contributors in most instances seem to us almost too local ; *i.e.*, however well they know 'Broad Norfolk,' they are not fully aware of modes of speech outside the county, and hence many of the words cited are not specially East Anglian. Thus, in Mr. Giles's ' article alone we find *clamber, tantrums, ingen* (=*onion*)*, pig's chitterlings, gobs* (of fat, *cf.* Spencer's *gobblets raw*)*, mittens, highlows, bunny, mavis* (= *thrush*)*,* and that word of queer history, *sisserary,* spelt also *susserara,* and in other ways : One boy will give another ' a *clip* o' the head,' or '*a souse* o' the skull;' and I once heard a fellow say he had given another a *sisserary—*evidently a rather astonishing blow. The word was, in fact, in use, though rarely, among our eighteenth-century writers, and we ourselves heard it used not infrequently in London, now, alas ! about forty years ago ; it then meant a thundering rat-tat-tat at one's front door. In the letters before as we find *game leg, shortening* (for pie-crust), *gaffer,* (contracted from *grandfather,* just as *gammer* from *grandmother,* a *t'do, keep squat, pax-wax, play the Charley, slack-baked, feyther* (as in Lancashire), a *tidy lot,* and others, which will be familiar to our readers.

"Secondly, some of the contributors' conjectural explanations do not quite suit. Thus, Mr. 'Giles's remaks that 'in Suffolk houses are called *housen,* which is perhaps the old Saxon form'; but it isn't the old Teutonic plur. of *hûs* was *hûsa,* and the final *a* dropt off in Anglo-Saxon, making sing. and plur. alike. The abnormal *en*-plur. sprang up much later, and was formed by assimilation to other *en*-plurals, like *eyen*, *oxen*, &c. So again he speaks of *troat*, *tree*, *trow*, &c., for *throat*, *three*, &c., as caused by dropping an *h*; but the *h* in *th* is only a part of a clumsy contrivance for representing a *simple* sound; what really happens is that the 'South Folk' substitute the tenuis or hard closed mute for the related open spirant: there is no separate *h* in speaking. As a similar substitution has taken place in modern Scandinavian dialects, it is a very interesting question whether Scandinavian influence may not have affected the Suffolk pronunciation.

"From the many genuinely local words cited we will refer to two or three only:—*Hutkin* (a 'finger-stall' or 'cot' put over a sore or cut may mean 'a little *hat* or cap'; it has an oddly German look (as if=*Hut* plus suffix-chen). *Snaasty* may perhaps throw light upon our unexplained *nasty*; it means 'nasty-tempered.' Lastly, *fare* and *toward* (saw *tow'-ard*, 'well-disposed,' &c., the opposite of *fro-ward*) are cited by several correspondents. Says one: 'I once cautioned an ostler to be careful how he took out my mare; whereupon he patted her on the neck, and said: "She *fare toward like tho*," which the writer translates as 'She *appears to be* quiet and gentle.' *Fare*, therefore, as it seems to us, may be for *fa'er*, from *fav'r* = *favour* (*cf.* our *e'er*, for *ever*; *poor*, Chaucer's *pore* for *povre*, French *pauvre*, Latin *pauper-em*); and *fare* for *favour*, would mean *to be like*, *look like*; as in Lancashire, 'He *favours* his feyther,' &c.; the ostler's answer would thus strictly mean, 'She *looks like* a toward animal.' One should trace the history of the word, however, if possible, before pronouncing a decision.

"We can at present say no more, except that the *Norfolk News* and its contributors are earning the thanks of all dialect investigators."

THE END.

www.ingramcontent.com/pod-product-compliance
Lightning Source LLC
Chambersburg PA
CBHW020131170426
43199CB00010B/715